Why take the scenic route to success? Jumpstart your future— without going to college!

Accelerate your career without a college degree by finding your motivation and tapping into non-traditional learning opportunities. Others have done it, and so can you. In REAL WORLD CAREERS, you'll learn from the experiences of people like:

- **The Entrepreneur.** The daughter of hippies, Dana Korey didn't enter a classroom until the second grade. After struggling through high school, she quit college early. Now she runs her own business—with annual sales of $750,000.
- **The Sales Wiz.** "I was 6'4" and had an attitude," says Chet Holmes. In the tenth grade, a fistfight got him thrown out of school. Now this high-school dropout is a successful performance consultant whose advice has doubled and tripled sales for dozens of companies.
- **The Master Chef.** At sixteen, Ken Addington entered a city internship program that sparked his interest in food. He skipped cooking school in favor of an apprenticeship— and now makes close to six figures a year as an executive chef at a trendy New York restaurant.
- **The Manager.** Kristin Crockett's enthusiasm plummets in the classroom, but in the real world, she's a dynamo. After leaving college early and starting a low-level job, she rose rapidly through her company ranks, eventually becoming the benefits manager—for 4,000

◆ **The Millionaire**. Tim Jordan's parents stopped paying for school when it became clear he wasn't focused. Ten years later, he had worked his way up in the mortgage business—and become a millionaire in the process.

"Without dismissing college as a means to learn and grow, this stimulating book shows proven alternatives for getting rich without a college education. Anyone looking for guidance and resources needs to get this book. It would make a great gift for the kids you care about—as well as for yourself."

—Joe Vitale, author of *The Attractor Factor* and *Life's Missing Instruction Manual*

Real World Careers

Why College Is Not the Only Path to Becoming Rich

BETSY CUMMINGS

WARNER
BUSINESS
BOOKS™

NEW YORK   BOSTON

The information in this book is as up to date as possible, however, it is sold with the understanding that such information is often subject to new and changing interpretations, government rulings, and legislation. The reader should seek qualified professional help regarding specific questions.

Copyright © 2007 by Betsy Cummings

Warner Business Books
Hachette Book Group USA
1271 Avenue of the Americas
New York, NY 10020

Visit our Web site at www.HachetteBookGroupUSA.com

Warner Business Books is an imprint of Warner Books, Inc.

Printed in the United States of America

First Edition: January 2007

10 9 8 7 6 5 4 3 2 1

Warner Business Books is a trademark of Time Warner Inc. or an affiliated company. Used under license by Hachette Book Group USA, which is not affiliated with Time Warner Inc.

Library of Congress Cataloging-in-Publication Data

Cummings, Betsy.
    Real world careers: why college is not the only path to becoming rich/Betsy Cummings.—1st ed.
        p. cm.
    Includes index.
    ISBN-13: 978-0-446-69803-0
    ISBN-10: 0-446-69803-2
    1. Career development. 2. Vocational guidance. 3. Success in business. I. Title.
    HF5381.C885 2007
    650.14—dc22   2006019164

Book design and text composition by Stratford Publishing Services, Inc.

Acknowledgments

I would like to thank Dan Ambrosio and Rick Wolff, my editors at Warner Business Books, who gave me the opportunity to explore such a rich subject. As an author, the career paths of noncollege grads is no small topic to tackle when you consider the myriad job options for Americans who choose such a track. In that sense, my editors helped me formulate, define, and create a robust resource for those job seekers who don't have a college degree but have so much else to offer today's workplace.

Many thanks to experts Ron Krannich, Josh Flowerman, Bruce Palmer, Jim Zuberbuhler, Lou Glazer, Debra Humphreys, Dan Miller of Monster, and others who shed so much light on the job market and opportunities available for those without college degrees. The resources available online and through the U.S. Department of Labor were extraordinary in their data.

A huge thank-you to Marty Nemko, who provided tremendous insight and frank opinions about the value of a college education today.

Amy Barth was instrumental in shedding light on why high school students aren't focused enough on their career options—and how they could take better advantage of the resources at their fingertips.

Richard Weinblatt, Bob Webb, and Beth Youhn provided honest information about the opportunities and challenges today's blue-collar fields offer for both men and women. Personally, I never considered a path other than college when I entered a four-year university program twenty years ago. Today I certainly would. The reason? The stories provided by plenty of people interviewed for this book make clear that there are other options besides a bachelor's degree. This book would never have been possible without their input and insights. I certainly hope their stories are as inspiring to readers as they are to me. Those I interviewed over the past year demonstrate that a bachelor's degree is, indeed, not the only path to becoming rich.

Contents

The College Alternative

This year, more than sixteen million people will be enrolled in American colleges. Some will go because they want to. Others will be compelled by their parents. Far more will enter one of the country's four-thousand-plus institutions of higher education simply because they have no better plan. In fact, the number of students heading off to college increases each year, according to the National Center for Education Statistics; it rose by 15 percent between 1992 and 2002.

And what will they get for their four years of academic dedication? A few will launch promising careers. Many more will come out as clueless as they went in—uncertain of what inspires them or where their professional talents lie. They'll trundle off to countless interviews for low-level entry positions that may or may not promise a gateway to higher earnings and more responsibility. Others will take their crisp new hundred-thousand-dollar diplomas and land the jobs so often filled by thousands of graduates each year, working in stores or restaurants, for example, while they figure out what it is they really want to do with their bachelor's degrees.

But that's for those who even make it through. More than a quarter will drop out after year one. More than half won't graduate after five years. Many will be like Tim Jordan, an ambitious, hardworking individual motivated by money and success, but not by the structured, lecture-based setup of a classroom, trapped in an educational setting that's not appropriate for him. Jordan, who started at the University of Hartford ("not Harvard," he jokes) in Connecticut, called it quits on higher education two years later after transferring to a community college near home, then later the University of Maryland. "I took a class here and there but never followed through," Jordan says. "I was just having a good time." He is now a millionaire (see chapter 1), but not because of a college degree.

Like many who left the classrooms of higher education, Jordan is driven more by practical experience. College for him was a demoralizing exercise that only slowed him down. Too many people like Jordan waste years wandering aimlessly through esteemed university corridors, never focusing on a specific career or course of study. "By the time I left, I should have graduated twice," he says, "but I didn't."

Who should go to college? Probably only those whose legal, medical, and educational careers demand that they do. Or those who simply love to learn in an academic setting. "We genuflect before higher education as being this nonprofit opportunity to grow the mind and become a connoisseur of learning and all this high-minded stuff," says Marty Nemko, a career consultant and co-author of Cool Careers for Dummies. "In reality that is simply not the case. When you pull the curtain away from the PR rhetoric colleges put out nonstop and look at what kids learn... the amount of critical-thinking skills is paltry [next] to the amount of money and time" spent on a four-year program.

Finding the Right Payoff

Nemko's right. Part of the problem is society and the ridiculously high expectations it holds aloft for college grads. But why is college so highly valued when the statistics reveal that only a quarter of Americans even have college degrees? "In a country where we could provide college to every student, that's an opportunity we shouldn't squander," argues Debra Humphreys, vice president for communications and public affairs at the Association of American Colleges and Universities in Washington.

If you look at salary surveys, Humphreys's point bears out. In 2003, average college graduates earned 62 percent more than their peers with just a high school degree—a huge jump from 1972, when college graduates made 22 percent more than those with a high school diploma alone. Indeed, reports about everything from obesity to socioeconomic status continually weigh out in favor of those with bachelor's degrees.

But dozens of college dropouts interviewed for this book as well as those who sidestepped college entirely will argue otherwise. And they have the careers to prove it. Very few regret their decision to walk away from four-year programs. And all will tell you that getting a jump start on their career was extremely motivating.

If you're just finishing high school, have some work experience but no college degree, or simply never wanted to attend a university but are interested in making money, you may not be aware of just how lucrative a career can be for people who don't have a four-year diploma.

Consider Greg Brooks, a self-described victim of attention deficit disorder ("I had ADD before it was cool," he jokes). Brooks propelled his way through an ambitious journalism career after dropping out of college shortly after starting. Instead of burying his nose in his studies, Brooks pursued the communications field relentlessly, moving through a multitude of journalism jobs before finally landing in public relations. "I was an absolutely unrepentant job-hopper," he says. Today he owns his own public relations and marketing company, called West Third Group, located in Plattsburg, Missouri, and pulls in a comfortable quarter million dollars or more in business a year.

Or look at Ed Richards, who may not have a college degree but has seen and experienced plenty—even on college campuses. One of his first reporting assignments for a local radio station was to cover a burning building on the campus at Kent State University in Ohio. Initially the event seemed likely to fizzle, and Richards and other reporters quickly assumed the worst was over. "Some reporters said, this could go on all day, let's get lunch," Richards recalls. Turns out that small burning building was actually part of the Kent State riots, a protest poorly managed by the National Guard, which fired into the crowd of protestors, injuring thirteen and killing four. Just as the reporters headed off to lunch, the event's most horrific moments unfolded. "That was my first outside reporting job. I really didn't understand what the hell was going on," Richards says. "I just started running around and talking to people asking, 'What did you see? What happened?' I got a lot of great sound that day." Richards received his reporting baptism by fire from that day and built a radio career that spanned more than two decades.

Still not convinced? Listen to Terri Nopp, who says, "I have not found the lack of a degree limiting in any way." Her sentiments are shared by many in her position. Nopp came from a family of educators but realized after some time in college that higher education just wasn't for her. It didn't stop her from aspiring to and obtaining a highly lucrative career, however: Today she runs her own public relations firm billing more than half a million dollars a year to clients.

All these stories attest to one unequivocal career truth: A college degree is not necessary for success. Companies that remain enamored with the bachelor's degree are still out there, unfortunately, refusing to consider the (sometimes superior) talents of those without a four-year degree. "I look at the way we do things and it annoys me because I think we cut ourselves off from so many good people who didn't go to the right school or have the right internship," says one financial executive, who has attained astounding success in banking without a college degree. And while her company refuses to interview interns or other job applicants who aren't in the "correct" school, much less those without a bachelor's degree, this successful non-college-grad realizes the valuable workers the firm may be missing out on due to its policy. "I think it does an injustice" to her company and others with similar requirements for employment, she says.

Why College Doesn't Pan Out

The reality is, plenty—in fact many—of today's top workers, as well as those coming down the job market pipeline, just simply don't see college as a good fit in their lives. Why does college not work for so many who enroll? Experts point to youth's major stumbling block today: a lack of focus, particularly among high school graduates. In a thoroughly researched tome, *Unfocused Kids*, Suzy Mygatt Wakefield, PhD—a retired high school guidance counselor and career development facilitator who served as one of the book's editors—talks about the undefined gap many of today's young adults fall into, causing them to lack career focus. Wakefield writes: "When school becomes too difficult or they fall behind in credits, many of these teens tend to drop out of school—with the consequence of qualifying only for low-skilled, low-paying, dead end jobs. On the other hand, just going to college does not necessarily mean that teens will be successful either." Wakefield's right. High school graduates who aren't focused on a specific career won't necessarily find that focal point in college. More to the point, it can be an expensive place to meander through a trial-and-error curriculum, hoping you'll hit upon a program that sparks your interest. And when you consider that much of the nation's jobs can be had through certificate programs, apprenticeships, and on-the-job training, where employees are often paid to learn, slogging through a four-year degree simply doesn't make sense.

"The real growth has been in junior colleges with certification programs," says Ron Krannich, author and publisher of Impact Publications in Manassas Park, Virginia, which publishes dozens of business and career books. And apparently companies agree. According to the National Profile of Community Colleges: Trends and Statistics, a study put out by the American Association of Community Colleges, 95 percent of businesses that use education programs at community colleges, where the average student is twenty-nine, recommend such programs to others.

The point is not to hightail it out of high school at eighteen and launch randomly into a career. For those who bypass college, finding success is almost always the result of going through a focused, defined, productive educational and professional track. It's just that college isn't the only way to make that happen.

Who's Skipping School?

"There are two kinds of people who should forgo college," says Marty Nemko. "One is the real go-getter who is quite entrepreneurial." The second? "The zillions of non-academic-oriented students who can get into college, because colleges will take anyone."

For parents and teenagers too caught up in the prestige of having children with bachelor's degrees, skipping college entirely can seem like a daunting choice, particularly when those who decide to forgo a college education defy family expectations. Two years into her college career at Howard University in Atlanta, Kat Carney, who had a full scholarship, decided to walk away. "I came from a family of educators, so I believe in education and the value of it," says Carney, who received books every year for Christmas growing up. "It was so woven into the fabric of daily life" in her family, it's no surprise that her parents were devastated when she quit school to pursue an acting career. But Carney never felt college was the best path for her. "My parents definitely wanted me to go to college," she says; "if not for them I probably wouldn't have thought about applying to college or going." While at Howard, however, she kept thinking about how she wanted to be out experiencing the world, not sitting in a classroom learning about it.

Not that opting out of a university should be considered lightly. Certainly a college degree is necessary for some jobs and can open doors at plenty of companies. But an overwhelming amount of evidence exists in companies of all sizes and within nearly every industry that a college degree is frequently not necessary. Still, before saying good-bye forever to academia, it's important to truly determine if college is right for you or not.

Doing so should start with asking some of the following questions:

- ◆ Is your academic track record consistent? If it was spotty in high school, it will probably continue that way in college. Why pour thousands of dollars into an academic effort that's going to be lukewarm at best?

- ◆ Have your grades gone up or down in recent years? If they're on a downward slope, that's a sign that you're seriously uninspired by the classroom setting. It doesn't mean that you lack the brain power to make great grades. But sitting in a college classroom with gentlemen's C's will probably only kill what professional motivation you have left.

- ◆ Are you a strong test taker? Do your SAT scores reflect that? Performance tests such as SATs are a great indicator of future performance in an academic setting. If your scores are low, but your high school GPA is high, that says one thing. But average grades combined with average scores probably mean you're better off outside a university setting.

- ◆ Does the thought of leaving home leave you cold? Many students trudge off to college and are shocked by the intensity of their depression and homesickness. For many, this is the first time away from home, struggling with independence. Individuals strongly affected by home separation might want to explore job opportunities closer to home.

- ◆ Are you task-oriented and organized when studying, or are you easily distracted? If you're likely to roam your dorm hallways scavenging for pizza rather than sitting down and spending hours on end focused on your books, you may not have the discipline at the moment to be a great student. Ignore that reality and you'll likely sink thousands into costly tuition with a poor academic return for your investment.

◆ Do you find the classroom setting stifling? Ultimately, if you simply hate sitting and listening to teachers talk, or absorbing mass quantities of information, now's the time to admit it to yourself and get out. You're doing yourself and the school a disservice by being there.

◆ Are you passionate about any particular subject of study? If nothing turns you on, drop that college application immediately. Spending a year away from school trying to figure out what it is that could turn you on for an entire career is a far better use of your time.

◆ Do you have a clear image of what your career or next job will look like? If not, you probably won't pick up that vision by listening to your college art history professor. You'd be smarter to sink a few hundred dollars into the services of a career counselor or skills assessment testing center to figure out where your hidden talents lie.

These are obvious questions with black-and-white answers. But too often, young adults fail to ask them and blindly trust that their future will magically lead them down a straight and narrow path from within the college system. But without a clear picture of what lies ahead, far too many students become distracted by the lifestyle and nonacademic elements that accompany the college experience. "When students drop out of college, it's not because of what they're doing in class, but because they aren't handling the other pieces of college," says Jim Zuberbuhler, executive director of Dynamy, a thirty-seven-year-old organization that offers internships to students who want to take a gap year between high school and college, or want to spend time interning in a few professions to determine what might interest them most.

A Changing Work World

Even for those who aren't entirely certain of what they want to do, an expanding job market may work in their favor in the coming years, with or without a college degree to help open doors. In twenty years, seventy-six million baby boomers will retire. Many will return to the workforce in some capacity. But their departure will spark a major shift in corporate America's need to fill vacancies. When that happens, college degrees may seem less important to employers than specific skill sets and certifications. Already, "I think employers, smart employers, look at skills and things that need to be done on the job and less so at formal education," Ron Krannich says. "Employers are trying to hire your future rather than your past. They want to look at your performance: Are you trainable? Can you learn?"

Population shifts may be working in the favor of certain groups. For example, the number of females in the labor pool is expected to grow by 10.9 percent from 2001 to 2014, while the number of men in the labor market is expected to increase by only 9.1 percent, according to the US Bureau of Labor Statistics. For women, that may mean not only a greater takeover of jobs typically occupied more by men but a decrease in the earnings gap, which has generally shown that women make 75 percent of their male counterparts.

So who should skip school and who should pursue a four-year degree? Some of those answers are obvious, particularly if your career choice—as a lawyer or doctor, for example—requires extensive education. But plenty of occupations, including many in the medical and technology fields, require only technical training or an associate's degree.

For others not sure of what industry or type of career they'd like to follow, college may not provide the answers. Moving aimlessly through college classrooms is often not a productive means to figuring out your professional goals. In fact, experts often agree that, especially if you're a recent high school graduate, a year or two on your own after high school can help clear your mind professionally, sharpen your career focus, and increase your work ethic.

For others, the military, a vocational school, or even an apprenticeship may be a much smarter and more direct path to a career than a four-year degree. For those hoping to start a business in particular, taking a few classes in accounting or marketing at a local college is likely a far more productive (not to mention cheaper) route than plunking tens of thousands of dollars into a university's coffers.

And with a greater diversity of industries and companies needing talent, more and more may lessen position requirements when it comes to level of education completed. According to the Bureau of Labor Statistics, certain industries are expected to see vast growth until at least the year 2014, and thus need a greater number of employees in the next decade. These industries will represent great opportunity for all job seekers, and particularly so for those without a four-year degree.

XX   INTRODUCTION

HIGH GROWTH INDUSTRIES

Industry	Expected Growth
Health care and social assistance	30.3 percent
Professional and business services	27.8 percent
Information and Web industries	11.6 percent
Leisure and hospitality	17.7 percent
Trade, transportation, and utilities	10.3 percent
Financial industries	10.5 percent
Government	10 percent

Source: US Bureau of Labor Statistics

Figuring Out a Path

While some people interviewed for this book attended some school, others skipped college entirely; still others decided a trade school was the best way to forge a career. One person spent only a few years of her life in school, since her parents neglected to introduce her to any type of formal education until the age of ten. With that background, "I never viewed not going to college as a deficit," she says.

Although some people may think a college degree opens more doors initially, those who have skipped the four-year degree and found success in their careers disagree. "I started thinking about the return on my investment and how many years I would have to work to get a return" for the money invested in tuition, says Terri Nopp, who spun her wheels for three years at colleges in Arizona before finally realizing it wasn't helping her make headway down a professional path. Within "the field I was most interested in—which is architecture—the return would have taken twenty years!" Instead, she decided to pursue marketing and communications on her own. And not having a four-year degree hasn't prevented her from gaining top jobs or making six figures: "It's all about how smart you are, how quickly you adapt, and how you take advantage of any opportunities thrown your way."

Real World Careers

PART I

Closing the Books

Chapter One

Why College Makes No Sense

Tim Jordan never planned on enrolling at a university for seven years. But if he had continued down the academic path he began in the early 1990s, that's about how long it would have taken him to earn a college degree. "I didn't have a focus for school," he says, in an understatement.

When three years of study left him with a solid C average and an accumulation of credits alarmingly short of what he needed to graduate, his parents finally cut him off. "They pretty much said they didn't plan on me going to school for seven years," Jordan says. That was in 1991. In college, Jordan and a friend had started a small business doing odd construction jobs around town—fixing a porch deck here, repairing a fence there. It was enough to bring in forty thousand dollars a year, and lay a foundation of construction skills. But it was also an indication that money could be made without a bachelor's degree.

So when Jordan had a falling-out with his partner, he left the business and school at the same time, hoping to jump-start his career with the knowledge he'd gained to date. He landed a job as a hospital maintenance worker in Morristown, New Jersey.

Not the most auspicious start, perhaps. But a year later, still loping along in that position, Jordan was open to other options and was eager to listen to a friend who suggested he consider a new career. One day during a community softball game, that friend approached Jordan with a proposition. "He was in the mortgage business," Jordan relates. "He said, 'You know so many people. Why don't you give it a shot?'"

Jordan was as familiar with mortgages as he was with college commencement. But he decided to find out more. And here's where his motivation—inspired by life experience, rather than the classroom—kicked in. In a business where pay is 100 percent commission, a newcomer like Jordan couldn't afford to quit his day job, so to speak, and launch into another one sight unseen. He was terrified to commit solely to becoming a broker, but with a full-time job that offered an uncertain career path, he figured he had nothing to lose. So he continued to work his hospital maintenance job while he spent his nights at home as a representative for Central Mortgage Service Corporation, dialing one number after another, hitting up area residents who might be in the market for mortgages. Unable to make cold calls during the day, Jordan hired a telemarketing firm to do the work for him, then would take the contacts they drummed up and spend four hours a night working warm leads.

Jordan knew it was crucial to land his first customer—most mortgage clients are drawn in through referrals. But he didn't know when that would be. Patience and determination were crucial to making it happen. His very first client, it turns out, was one of his best friends. That certainly generated some referral business. But it didn't guarantee the stream Jordan had hoped for. And the company wasn't necessarily paving the way. "They threw me to the wolves," he says of his first employer.

"I had no idea what I was doing." Sitting in the home of one of his earliest prospects one night, Jordan recalls thinking he wasn't leaving without asking for and getting the business. "I was twenty-five years old and this lady is thirty-eight with kids, looking at me trying to sell her a mortgage," Jordan recalls, laughing. "She knew I was trying so hard. I was in her house for two and a half hours. I was not leaving that house without that mortgage." The woman was impressed with Jordan's initiative and was willing to use him as her broker. She just needed to ask him one final question: "Does this mortgage require an escrow?" Jordan stopped cold. "I had no idea what those were." But he wasn't about to lose the business. He took a chance and told her he was sure his company could provide escrow services should her mortgage need them. Turns out, his company could.

For a solid six months Jordan scrambled, educating himself about escrows and everything else he needed to know along the way. He continued to work nearly forty-hour weeks at the hospital, spending nights and weekends securing mortgages. The struggle paid off. In less than ten years, Jordan built his practice into a three-thousand-client business that averages a million dollars a year.

In that time, he worked for two different mortgage companies before becoming a partner in a third and building it into such a large entity, it was acquired in 2005 by another firm for sixteen million—much of that landing in Jordan's pocket. Going to college, Jordan says, served little purpose in launching his career other than building a few contacts to help spread the word about his mortgage broker services. "I could have probably gotten A's, but my attention span for focusing on school… it was never the environment in which I learn," Jordan says. "I am 100 percent money-motivated."

The Right Motivation

Like Jordan, too many college students don't find the motivation, inspiration, or career momentum they're looking for in a university lecture hall. Isn't it better to recognize that early in your academic career and find another path than it would be to spend four years hauling through analytical geometry or introduction to digital architecture, waiting for the moment of inspiration?

That Jordan skipped college and found vast financial and professional wealth is surely an anomaly, right? Wrong. Certainly four-year graduates with new diplomas and hundreds of credit hours sweating it out over calculus equations and quantum physics theorems have plenty of job opportunities ahead of them. But studies reveal a somewhat pessimistic future for many college undergraduates—or at least for those who finish. A recent survey by the Web site CollegeGrad.com found that more than half of all college graduates feel it's more difficult to find a job today than it was a year ago. A similar survey by the same site found that nearly 20 percent of college graduates said they were underemployed, complaining that even entry-level jobs can require some experience—a vicious catch-22 that frustrates recent grads.

College advocates say a degree can give you the mental boost needed when looking for a job. If you have a diploma, the theory goes, then surely you have the skills and talent to be a solid performer. And that builds confidence for newbies on the job. But plenty of college graduates leave school knowing full well that the slip of paper in their hands doesn't guarantee their success—or attest to their true abilities or intelligence. And their peers who have spent the last four years working and gaining bankable skills on the job may have far more to offer.

Making It Through

That, of course, is if they even make it through a full, four-year program, which plenty do not. Only about half of all college entrants actually walk out the other side with a degree, according to the latest numbers from ACT, a national education assessment and testing organization.

The top reason why those who enter college leave before they earn a degree? Lack of motivation. "There is this enormous pressure from all points in society that says you're a failure if you don't go off to college," Jim Zuberbuhler says. That's a dangerous message to send to those not ready today, or ever, for the college experience. It would be far more productive to focus on the best educational path for an individual, whether it's a vocational program or an apprenticeship. "All of us know people in our daily lives who are doing fine that don't have a four-year degree," says Lou Glazer, president of Michigan Future Inc., a civic organization in Ann Arbor, Michigan. "A four-year degree is a pathway but not the only pathway to a good paying career. Ingenuity matters. Drive matters. None of those things require a four-year degree."

Indeed they don't. Dozens of people interviewed for this book who skipped college or withdrew after a semester or more would agree. "The college experience, the way the classes were structured, it didn't fit my needs," says Ethan Smith, an information technology specialist who is on a fast track to a six-figure income after leaving school several years ago to pursue a computer career through certification programs. That path, he says, propelled him through his career faster and more effectively than a four-year computer science degree. As he puts it without regret: "I took a leave and never went back."

Worth the Cost?

What people like Smith and others are realizing is that the return on a college education doesn't always equal the money invested. A college degree today can range anywhere from fifty to upward of two hundred thousand dollars, depending on where a student attends school and for how long. The good news is that nearly 80 percent of full-time undergraduates pay less than eight thousand dollars a year in tuition, according to numbers from the American Council on Education. But given recent revenue short-falls in many states, legislators are looking to colleges to make up the slack; more than forty states have considered tuition increases at public institutions in the past few years. Still, even if the majority of tuition rates remained below ten thousand a year, that's a lot of money to drop just to dawdle while trying to figure out a career plan—especially since many who fork over such sums may not even land the job they want.

Financially, socially, professionally—there are many reasons to attain a four-year degree, says AACU's Humphreys. "The economic data is quite clear that any decent job that will pay you enough money to have a middle-class life will require some college in the future."

For some, maybe. But plenty of naysayers, including even college professors, note that a college degree is only important for those who are either educationally driven, become inspired in classroom settings, are pursuing careers that require formal education, or simply don't view any alternative as a better path than a university degree. The reality, say those critical of the all-college, all-the-time mentality, is that college is too hyped as the only means to a successful, lucrative career—a line of thinking that some insist simply isn't true. "Is college important?" asks

Marty Nemko. "For many people, yes." But Nemko, who holds a PhD and has taught or consulted at fifteen colleges, adds that for many others, college is simply not the best path to the career they want to pursue. "The more of a self-starter you are, the more of a competitive go-getter you are, the less you need college."

Plenty of students—"real winners," according to Nemko—learn far better and faster outside school by following the lessons of mentors on the job or in a professional environment of some type, rather than the classroom.

Indeed, Nemko and others who are outspoken critics of higher education suggest that college classrooms are quite often filled by people who are unmotivated, unfocused, or simply have no clue about what type of career they would like to pursue. That may be an unfair assessment of the nation's institutions of higher education. But it is sadly the reality for plenty of students, for whom entering college is the only acceptable choice among family and peers.

Proponents point to the interpersonal skills developed in college as crucial. College affords an important transition for students whose interpersonal skills or level of maturity aren't developed enough to handle work after high school graduation. Still, many contend that unless students are spending time among Ivy League students, they're hanging out with unmotivated undergrads just like themselves. And that, it's argued, is not an experience that will cultivate their intellect or help them grow professionally. Says Nemko, "Ninety-eight percent of colleges do not have Harvard-caliber students"—who can positively affect or influence incoming freshmen with their talent and ambition. "To pay two hundred thousand dollars for an institution that has just plain folk doesn't sound like a hell of an investment, not to mention four or five or six years of your time."

A SNAPSHOT OF US COLLEGE ENROLLMENT

Students in college today	16.6 million
Students in college 10 years ago	14.4 million
Students in college aged 25 and over	6.1 million
Female students in college	9.3 million
Caucasian students in college	11.3 million
Black students in college	2.2 million
Asian students in college	1.2 million
Hispanic students in college	1.7 million

Source: US Census Bureau, 2003

Is College for You?

From almost the first day of elementary school, students are propelled along a trajectory that, for many, includes focusing on GPAs, SATs, honors classes, college admissions, and anxious waiting periods where high school students sweat it out hoping to get into the school of their choice. College enrollment figures reflect this, with the number of students enrolled in higher education nationwide rising by more than two million students in the past decade, according to census figures. Of course, some of this can be attributed to an increase in population among Americans in traditional college-aged groups, eighteen to twenty-four, over the past decade, but others contend that many more students are simply feeling that a college education behind them is a guarantee for a better job with a higher salary.

And why wouldn't they? Plenty of statistics indicate that as well. According to the College Board, an organization in New York that promotes college connections for students, in 2003 a full-time worker in the United States made a median income of $49,900 while the same worker with only a high school diploma made $30,800.

For every person who bears out such statistics, however, there are counterexamples of people who have decided to forgo college and find their way to higher earnings by some other means. The real message here, say educators and experts, is that high school graduates shouldn't feel that college is the only path for them. And even for nearly seventeen million students who seem destined for the road to college, the idea of a four-year program can seem unappealing or depressing.

"I went for a semester and I couldn't deal," says Kristin Crockett, manager of training for Qwest Communications International Inc., a telecommunications company based in Denver. "I was never a big fan of school in general."

To Campus or Not?

How do you know if college is right for you? For some people, it's instinctual. "My mother owned a bookstore while I was growing up. And my father was a colonel in the army. They definitely wanted me to go to college," says Kat Carney, who nevertheless felt so strongly that college wasn't for her that she threw away her full scholarship to Howard University. She exhibited all the signs of someone seemingly college-bound. "My grades were better than average. My SATs were really, really, really good. On math I was twenty points off of a perfect score. But I realized I was just never all that driven to go to college."

Entering with an undeclared major, then later focusing on hotel administration, Carney eventually left to pursue acting; she went on to a successful career as a CNN health anchor and host on QVC. Like many before and after her, Carney realized early on that sitting in a classroom is not only uninspiring, but can actually kill motivation and enthusiasm for learning. For such people, college is simply not the best route to a career. And in some professions, such as trades, embarking on an apprenticeship, finding entry-level work, or enlisting the help of a mentor will do far more to propel you into a successful career than a piece of paper that attests to your ability to sit in a classroom, listen to lectures, study, and pass exams for four years straight—if you're lucky enough to get out in four years.

Too Little Thought, Too Late

Many educators say students aren't focusing on their post-high-school plans early enough, failing to consider what courses would best facilitate their desired career path in early high school or even late middle school. Repeated studies reveal a low reliance on many high school guidance departments, where counselors are being woefully underused to help high school students figure out which classes to take and where they might start focusing their professional aspirations. A 2002 survey by ACT, providers of the popular college entrance exam by the same name, revealed that only 22 percent of eighth- and ninth-grade students had thought about post-high-school plans. Thirteen and fourteen years old may seem young to be forging a career path, but the reality is that the earlier students explore careers, the more likely they are to develop a focused plan of attack. And finding the most educated, well-informed people to help do that is crucial as well. Too often students rely on family and friends to help them consider a profession of choice. While they can provide invaluable insight into your academic and interpersonal strengths and weaknesses, relying largely on family and friends can cloud your judgment. Parental career suggestions in particular can be fraught with bias and unhealthy expectations, as parents push children into careers they don't want to follow.

Looking for Answers

If you're going to tap those you know—such as your parents, siblings, and best friends—for career suggestions, just make sure you are eliciting advice, opinions, and career counseling from other sources as well. A great place to start: your high school guidance office (if you haven't graduated already). You'd also be wise to spend time with guidance counselors who can help administer career tests and exams that assess your skills and interests. Unfortunately, too few students do so.

WHERE STUDENTS LOOK FOR CAREER ADVICE

Mother	92 percent
Father	84 percent
Friends	85 percent
Guidance counselor	63 percent
School principal	27 percent

Source: ACT

Even for those who do tap the resources of high school guidance counselors or educational consultants, it's important at some point to honestly ask yourself if college is the best path to professional success.

Consider the following:

- ◆ Are you stimulated by classroom lectures or discussions with fellow students? If you don't make good grades now, a mediocre grade point average from a large state university isn't exactly going to put you on the fast track to executive status.
- ◆ Are you more inspired by physical or by intellectual activities? If classroom lectures don't do it for you, listening to a professor drone on—or worse, scoring poorly on all your exams—will probably flatten what little enthusiasm and energy you had going into a university.
- ◆ Are you a risk taker or more comfortable with tradition and certainty?
- ◆ Are you willing to embark on a career immediately after high school even if it means failing and deciding to enter college in your twenties or thirties?
- ◆ Is the financial commitment of college something you could easily cover or would getting a degree require taking out thousands of dollars in loans?
- ◆ Are you willing to break from family tradition and expectations that a college degree is crucial?
- ◆ Most importantly, do you have a clear vision of the career you want to pursue? If not, college is an expensive place to putter around debating your professional course.

The Value of College

When getting a bachelor's degree can cost close to a quarter million dollars, including books, tuition, room and board, and other expenses, many find it shocking how deficient college graduates are in academic skills. The most recent National Assessment of Adult Literacy by the US Department of Education, for instance, noted general declines in adult literacy among undergraduate and graduate students in the past decade. Literacy tasks—an indication of a person's employability—dropped as much as 10 percentage points in some categories, among them college graduates' ability to read and understand literature passages. And, according to ACT, one-third of undergraduates take remedial course work at some point in college.

Such shortcomings in students' reading comprehension may explain why a quarter of those who start college leave before getting a degree. One argument college students may find comforting: Studies do show that college graduates can generally expect higher earnings—as much as twice what nongraduates may make, according to the latest census figures. But what those numbers don't take into account are the people who saw college as an obstacle in their career paths. These go-getters avoided the experiences of their friends who graduated in four to six years, got out, and found themselves in low-paying entry-level jobs, often with huge student loans to pay back. Believe it. It happens. Far too many sad stories have been told of college graduates doing menial jobs. For every grad who lands a high-five-figure job on Wall Street, there are many more who end up waiting tables at Chili's or ringing up chinos at J.Crew.

More to the point, too many high school students are being oversold on the notion that college is the only way to professional success. That's a disservice to students when you consider that only half of those who enroll will actually go on to attain a four-year degree. Too many college enrollees attend a few classes only to realize that college is not for them. Plenty who have the initiative to walk away are finding success in their jobs when they do so. When Greg Brooks entered college in the mid-1980s, he did so with one eye on the door. Impatient sitting in classes day after day, Brooks was more into getting practical experience. Which explains why he left one college after another and finally ended up at a local daily newspaper begging for any job they would give him. He landed one doing page layout, and never looked back. "After a short number of weeks," Brooks says, "it was clear, what I was learning in school was not directly appropriate to what I was doing on a daily basis." In other words, college wasn't at all preparing him for the real world.

How Long Does It Take to Earn a College Degree?

Years	Men	Women	Total
4	32.6 percent	39.7 percent	36.3 percent
6	55.2 percent	59.6 percent	57.6 percent
6-plus	59 percent	62 percent	60.6 percent

Source: Degree Attainment Rates at American Colleges and Universities, Higher Education Research Institute, UCLA

A Job Market for Nongraduates

What today's non-college-graduates should consider is that the job market is likely about to swing in their favor, thanks to population and market shifts in coming years that may leave American businesses with a dearth of applicants for openings.

Baby boomers, for example, some seventy-six million of whom will be retiring in the next twenty years, will create a huge gap in the number of applicants versus openings in the job market—as many as five million, according to the Bureau of Labor Statistics. Their exit from corporate America will leave many companies scrambling to fill positions—a dilemma that might cause firms to drop educational requirements for jobs. "There is going to be a skills gap, clearly, as boomers retire," says Dan Miller, vice president of learning and development for the job search engine Monster.com. "And as an employer or hiring manager who has a very strong need" to fill a vacancy, "I'm more interested in someone who can do the job than whether or not they have the academia behind it."

That's not only in white-collar jobs. For those who think blue-collar and service jobs are all being outsourced overseas, think again. Yes, plenty are, but many more are staying here, and fields such as law enforcement, construction, and even maritime work are offering Americans without university diplomas a chance to enter a trade profession and experience rapid advancement.

In fact, Michigan Future Inc.'s Glazer estimates that only some "30 percent of jobs seem to require four-year degrees" today. Plenty of successful entrepreneurs, executives, medical professionals, politicians, designers, performers, and other individuals have created thriving careers without ever acquiring one college credit.

Finding the Right Path

The key, experts say, is forging the career path that makes most sense to an individual, and making the most of the skills he or she has. Kristin Crockett's enthusiasm plummets in the classroom.

Almost like a guaranteed inverse reaction, when an instructor speaks, Crockett deflates. "High school was a lot of fun," Crockett recalls, "but not academically. It was not my most favorite way to spend my time." Like so many high school students, Crockett wasn't exactly on the fast track to career superstardom. "I had no clue of what I wanted to study or what I wanted to do." Except that she wanted to stop throwing away thousands of dollars a semester into a college education that, as far as she could tell, was taking her nowhere.

"I learn best by experience," Crockett says. At college "I took this art history class, which I loved, but I didn't want to be tested on it. I wanted to go to Europe and see this stuff in person."

Uninspired by her degree program and unsure where to turn, she decided to talk to her father—who happened to be the president of a printing company in Colorado. Since school wasn't holding her interest, Crockett's father suggested that she try working instead. It seems strange that it took a small office manager role to light a fire under Crockett. But it did. "I just loved making money and the interaction with clients and the different lifestyle that came along" with earning money and having the freedom to make purchasing choices, Crockett says. "I was responsible for things and was able to see the results of my efforts."

Leaving college early rather than becoming burned out through a four-year degree was the propulsion for all her professional successes that followed.

Millions of Americans hold similar roles in offices across the country and never feel the giddy embrace of office freedom that Crockett discovered that day. But her subsequent rapid-fire rise through the human resource departments at multiple companies is evidence that opportunities are endless in corporate America, depending upon how well you exploit them.

After three years getting her feet wet at her father's printing company, Crockett moved on to a cable television firm in Denver. She was twenty-one. But transitioning from a small printing firm to a large cable provider meant she'd have to start at the bottom again—a lesson many without college degrees admit they've faced as they strategize ways to enter a career. Still, those who work long hours, contribute enthusiastically to their workplace, and ask repeatedly to be given more responsibility say that days toiling in reception level work is short-lived. That held true for Crockett as well. Her salary when she landed the job in 1985 was a barely-break-even twelve thousand dollars a year. But Crockett saw ample opportunity. After less than eighteen months on the job, she was promoted to human resource assistant. A year later, she was one of the company's benefits assistants. By 1993, she was the benefits manager for the entire company, managing health care and retirement plans for four thousand people.

At Jones Intercable, Inc., where she first landed a job as a receptionist, she threw her name in the hat for any job one or two positions above her for which she thought she was qualified. Within a year, she moved up to a small office management role in the company's HR department, and slowly went about taking on more and more responsibility. She identified slackers in the department and started offering to do tasks they might have let slide. Over time she gradually took on responsibilities that related to employee benefits, an area of human resources that interested her. Within a few years, she was managing the company's entire medical, dental, and retirement benefits suite as well as providing orientation seminars for new hires.

When the company implemented a diversity program, Crockett quickly became certified in diversity training and volunteered to implement the program. "I identified training as my passion and began to move into the training area," making it her specialty, Crockett says.

Crockett is by no means a poster child for focused teens barreling toward a specialized career path. After all, she meandered through what little college she attended, then stumbled into her father's printing company with "no clue," as she says, about her professional future. But she did have enough awareness to identify key stimulators that excited her professionally—specifically, making money, being responsible for others, and leading training sessions. That's enough to have a clear idea of where her work should take her.

And her lack of a college degree? It was rarely an issue. When the dreaded question did arise, Crockett was brutally honest. "If people ask me why I don't have a college degree, I say continuing my education wasn't one of my interests. And working was so interesting to me that I decided to follow that" right away.

Peddling the Non-College-Candidate

- ◆ **Do research.** Even if you don't like school, you're going to have to put some of the skills you picked up there to good use—namely, researching and studying careers that may be of interest to you. The good news: It's far more thrilling to submerge yourself in career assessment tools than algebraic formulas.
- ◆ **Have a sense of entitlement.** Just because you don't have a degree doesn't make you any less marketable or productive as an employee. Good employers know this, so keep it in mind. Remind yourself of it when on job interviews or whenever doubt creeps into your head

should you land a coveted job that has you working alongside an Ivy grad every day.

- ◆ **Match skill sets to jobs available.** Having a bachelor's degree under your belt doesn't necessarily add to the skills you possess naturally. Remember this, and figure out other ways to develop and exploit them—perhaps through adult education or on-the-job training.

- ◆ **Be aggressive.** "I would maneuver myself to be visible and available more so than just knocking down people's doors," Crockett says. Rather than hounding managers for random extra work, Crockett would identify key projects that the company might initiate that would interest her. Then she would approach the manager in charge and offer her assistance and ideas.

Like Crockett, Monster's Miller says, "Don't apologize" for not having a degree. "I know people here at Monster who don't have a college degree, and you wouldn't know it by the way they present themselves." Those without a bachelor's degree can do plenty to offset that missing credential on their résumé.

Quiz: Are You Ready for College?

Still not sure if college is the best path for you, even though your three older siblings have followed that course? Don't take tradition's path just for the sake of maintaining the status quo or to please Mom and Dad. Take the following quiz to see if college is the best place for you to advance your career. Keep in mind that your answers are an exercise in thinking about the best course for you. The following questions are not necessarily a replacement for a Myers-Briggs personality test or months with a career coach. But they are a great way to explore what is likely your best educational path.

If an academic subject interests me, I tend to:
a) Hope the instructor offers more information on that topic in the next class.
b) Take in the information I received in class that day and leave it at that.
c) Research the topic online in my own time.

When studying for a test, I often:
a) Force myself to sit down and study until I've covered all the material in one sitting.
b) Take mini breaks every fifteen minutes to avert the boredom of studying.
c) Cram at the last minute and hope for the best.

When I get a bad grade on a test or in a class, I:
a) Go to the instructor and try to figure out exactly where I made mistakes.
b) Accept that I did the best I could and vow to do better next time.
c) Lose all hope of catching up in class or boosting my final grade.

If I run into someone who knows more than I do, my first thought is:
a) This is great, I could really learn something from her.
b) If I act like I know what she's talking about, she'll think I'm smart.

c) I hate that I'm never as knowledgeable about ideas or news as everyone else.

When I think about moving away from home, my first thought is:
 a) Finally, I get to meet a fresh group of people who might offer new opportunity.
 b) That's scary, but I'll eventually adapt after a stressful period of acclimation.
 c) How will I cope without old friends and my family?

If someone asks me today what kind of job I want, I would:
 a) Rattle off a title and details of the job's responsibilities.
 b) Say I have a few in mind, but I'm not sure which one to pursue.
 c) Meet them with a blank stare and say I have no idea.

I just bought a new computer. It's not working, so I'm going to:
 a) Call the manufacturer's customer service line for help.
 b) Ask a friend who's technologically savvy to get it working.
 c) Experiment until I figure it out on my own.

If I had to pick one of the following professions, it would be:
 a) Lawyer or doctor.
 b) Advertising account executive.
 c) Entrepreneur.

If I'm cooking dinner for a friend, I:
 a) Use a recipe.
 b) Order food from a local restaurant.

c) Pull together a dish of my own from ingredients found in my kitchen.

My opinion of college is:
   a) It's a great way to stretch my mind and gain valuable skills for a job.
   b) It's a necessary step to the job market.
   c) I'd rather skip it.

Now count up your answers. Give yourself 2 points for every a) answer, 1 point for every time you answered b), and no points for c). If your score is 15 or higher, college is probably an ideal path for you. You respond well to structured learning situations and feel comfortable in them. Any score from 8 to 14 means college could be in your future, but you might want to either think more seriously about what exactly you hope to gain from four years of higher education, or take a year off and figure out more specifically what your career goals are and whether or not a four-year program is the key to accomplishing them. Any score below 8 means that your educational efforts and career spirit will likely be squandered on a college campus. You possess plenty of your own initiative to determine which career path is right for you, and you're more inspired in becoming educated outside of the traditional academic setting.

Chapter Two

A Different Route

For Chet Holmes, it started with a fight—a knock-down, drag-out, get-forever-suspended-from-school fight. "I was six foot four and had an attitude," says Holmes, a high school dropout who has gone on to double and triple sales for dozens of companies, and become a nationally recognized and highly sought-after sales and performance consultant. But back in the late 1970s, his education was coming to an end. Holmes, one of five children, was the son of a strict, unforgiving police officer and a nurturing housewife. By his second year of high school, he had been shuffled through eight schools, fighting students at each location. "We were poor...and I didn't give a crap about school," Holmes says. In fact, in his family, "there were no expectations for college." Apparently not. By tenth grade, he was thrown out for the last time after school officials expelled him for bad behavior and too many days absent from class. "My father said, 'Go ahead, I knew you were going to quit anyway.'"

So Holmes did. He left Middletown, New York, and his last classroom at Middletown High School, with twenty-five dollars.

With no place to go, he hitchhiked to Binghamton, New York, where a friend of his lived, only to find out once he got there that his friend had suffered a similar fate. He had been caught sniffing glue at school and subsequently been suspended. Hearing this, the father of Holmes's friend, fed up with his son's delinquency, kicked him out of the house. So when Holmes showed up at his friend's residence unannounced, he was told by the father that his friend was no longer living there. At the same time, the father had decided to move out as well, a strange, coincidental series of events that Holmes never quite sorted out.

What he had sorted out was that his options were dwindling fast. When he explained to his friend's father that he had arrived there seeking shelter, the father said the best he could offer was a small payment if Holmes would help him move. So Chet pitched in, netting another twenty-five bucks.

With that money he rented a room at a local hotel, "a Social Security hotel with roaches." A color TV in the lobby with faulty tubes broadcast programs in green. What Holmes had, though, was ambition and a strong work ethic, despite his bleak surroundings and irreverent attitude toward authority and rules. He landed a job as a hospital janitor, followed quickly by a position as the local movie theater's manager. "It paid crap, but you wore a tuxedo in those days," Holmes says, "so I thought I was cool."

One day, a patron approached him. "Someone said to me, 'You're very personable and outgoing. You should get into sales,'" Holmes says. With a week of vacation from the theater due to him, Holmes decided to use that time and investigate his aptitude for selling. It was a pivotal decision.

The moviegoer helped him land a brief job at a furniture store, which was the experience that changed Holmes's life.

He was mesmerized by the finesse with which his manager, John, sold thousands of dollars in furniture to the most unsuspecting clients. One day, "He walked over to a couple checking out recliners," Holmes says. "He said, 'You like this one?' The man says, 'Yeah.' John says, 'Where do you live?' The man says, 'Otisville.'" Holmes's manager's response: "We go there on Tuesday and Thursday. Which day is better for you?"

The customers were being blindsided with the manager's aggressive sales pitch, and Holmes was fascinated by the process. "They say, 'Tuesday,' and John starts to write up the order. I'm thinking, *Wow! He didn't even ask them if they wanted to buy.*" Holmes was hooked. "That was the beginning," he recognizes now, when he knew selling would be his career—mastering the art of persuading others to see the value of his pitch. From that point on, it didn't matter where he sold or what product or service he was peddling, it was the process of closing the deal that mattered most—and the more difficult the selling environment, the more Holmes rose to the challenge. At a personnel firm in New York, where long-term relationships shut out new sellers to the industry, Holmes knocked relentlessly on doors, focusing on big players such as CBS, until he managed to lock in one contact, then use that person as a gateway to others within the company. By nineteen, in the 1980s, he was making fifty thousand dollars a year interviewing and trying to place college graduates who couldn't find jobs.

For Holmes, the key to success was simple: "I didn't follow the rules in any place I ever worked."

Many who avoid the traditional structure of the university setting do so because they, like Holmes, want to follow a more unstructured, impassioned path that they feel offers opportunity in more places. For Holmes, school means "Don't talk in class, follow the rules, and make us function as a factory society." If he was to survive, getting out of the environment he found so stifling was the only way to achieve success. For some it works. Experts agree, suggesting that young adults who buck educational trends and skip college to pursue their own professional passion, much like Holmes, often find a quicker, more inspiring, more lucrative career path. But the real lesson that Holmes's story offers is the importance of identifying what passion drives you and pursuing that relentlessly once you find it. Miller of Monster.com says, "My suggestion for somebody who just does not have that degree is to really focus on what they're very good at" or what captivates their interest day in and day out.

Not sure what your greatest passion is? You're not alone. Many people wander passively through life, never fully recognizing their greatest zeal. That holds true particularly for the workplace. Think about what interests you day in and day out—outside your current job, if that's not a source of inspiration. What types of magazines or books do you read? What TV programs draw you in time and again? What well-known figures do you identify with? Perhaps their values or passions mirror yours. Almost any interest can be turned into a career or a way to make money. A recent article in *Kiplinger's* magazine recounted how one fire captain in New Jersey discovered his passion for building sand castles while playing with his children on the beach. Today he's an internationally renowned sand castle sculptor (and still a firefighter) who makes as much as eighty thousand dollars a year for his creations.

Being that impassioned about a subject leads to innovation on the job. When Holmes was charged with finding clients, he didn't put in his time cold-calling two hundred companies and routinely, mechanically asking if they needed temporary workers, as most of his colleagues did. Instead, he got smarter faster, identifying the top twenty-five companies in his area, then calling them relentlessly, working first on winning over receptionists, then moving on to more internal contacts until he gained referrals to each company's decision makers. Holmes went on to earn $250,000 a year by the age of twenty-seven and began his own business consultancy when he was thirty-one.

Today his sales consultancy, among other services, helps companies weed out the complacent job candidates by running them through prescreening drills over the phone. Too many recent college grads, Holmes says, are robotic order takers who simply put in their time selling without really knowing how to close the deal. Finding top performers—in any field—is done not on college campuses, according to experts such as Holmes, but by identifying those with a focus and passion for what they're doing.

A More Direct Path

Like Holmes, the best way to career success for many people is not via college, but straight into a job, whether directly after high school or shortly thereafter. Doing so gives young adults time to test-drive a few professions, so to speak, and figure out what truly inspires them. It also gives them a head start on their peers who are toiling away in classrooms memorizing mathematical formulas they may never use again.

The problem: Even responsible young adults in their twenties can easily get sidetracked by life when their career path doesn't have a focused future. When Kristin Crockett entered a community college straight out of high school, she should have known that it was a waste of time. But Crockett, who had "zero idea of what I wanted to do," decided not to launch into any particular career. Instead, she spent some time in her father's business developing a better sense of the specific industry she wanted to pursue. Both Holmes and Crockett, who wandered through jobs initially, eventually found their focus—and the road to professional motivation, success, and wealth. What can today's youth learn from their journeys?

Finding the Way

Trying to find the right career path? It can be daunting if your high school years weren't spent trying to find out what might spark your interest for an entire career. Welcome to the club. Few people spend their high school years or even the next ten after that seriously determining what it is that might turn them on professionally for a lifetime. As a result, they often languish in unfulfilling work. But that doesn't have to be the case. Finding the right career involves some routine questions and then some more that probe a little deeper.

Whether you're just leaving high school, have a year of college under your belt and don't want to return, or have been out in the workplace for ten years, consider the following while thinking about your next career move:

◆ **Passions.** It seems hokey, but it's harped about for a reason. People who find jobs that speak to their greatest passion are always the most fulfilled at work. How to figure out what lights your fire? Think about what you naturally gravitate toward for fun when you're not working. Think about how creative you like to be. What areas of school were always your best? Were there any particular subjects that turned you on in class? What do your family and friends always seem to count on you for?

♦ **Environment.** Are you more comfortable with your feet flat on the floor swiveling in an office chair inside a cubicle, for example, or is it vitally important to work outside?

♦ **Mode of work.** Do you enjoy working with your hands, or would you rather be a strategic thinker and leave the labor to others?

♦ **Travel.** Do you have a family or so much community involvement, say, that traveling for work would be anathema to you? Or are you willing to step on a plane once a week depending on where your job takes you?

♦ **Independence.** Do you work best alone, or will you shrivel up and call social hotlines just to hear a voice if you're not surrounded by at least ten people in a friendly office environment?

♦ **Pay.** Since this book is intended to point people toward more lucrative jobs, it's probably safe to assume that you're gunning for something more than minimum wage. But are you so impassioned about a particular line of work that you're willing to start on the bottom and earn next to nothing just to get in on the ground floor? Or is reaching the six-figure mark the most important point of your professional life? A note on income: Certainly some jobs pay better than others, which may be a deciding factor for some people. But deciding on a line of work simply because it offers great riches too often leads people to the poorhouse. When individuals are so impassioned about what they do that they work extra hours and throw themselves into their jobs, the money invariably follows. Picking a line of work for its interest is always smarter than picking a career for money alone.

Online Guides

Still don't have a clue about where your professional proclivities lie? There are a few Web sites to check out. One of the best is Career Voyages (www.careervoyages.com), a joint effort between the Departments of Labor and Education that offers information about hot careers with strong growth, as well as educational resources for getting started on a career search. Links on the site list dozens of URLs where visitors can take free self-assessment tests to gauge career interest, as well as gain access to numerous organizations, such as the National Career Development Association.

Other sites like 3SmartCubes.com (www.3smartcubes.com) and Tickle (web.tickle.com) offer free IQ and personality assessment tests, among other tools. How scientific these are is probably up for debate, but they are at least a legitimate starting point for assessing where your mental strengths and weaknesses lie.

One of the best career exploration sites available is probably O*NET Consortium (www.onetcenter.org), sponsored by the Department of Labor and RTI International, a nonprofit research organization. The site offers information on making career assessments, changes, and a comprehensive list of thousands of detailed job descriptions.

Finding the Alternative

Of the freshman who enter universities and colleges this year, nearly a quarter will never return. Many will become bored with the classroom setting and say they're too uninspired to come back. Others will say they are more compelled to start their career immediately. Still more will find it frustrating to rotate through an academic program when they aren't even sure what it is they want to do with their lives. And that, say experts, is the real problem with too many students who enter the university system.

So many people who rotate through Bernie Zimmerman's office exhibit the same characteristics: "Kids who drop out of high-profile schools because they're not being emotionally prepared for college," says Zimmerman, an educational consultant who works for Greenwood Associates in Tampa, Florida. Often these kids "have been in a sheltered home where Mom and Dad are doing everything for them." Suddenly they're sent off to college or out into the world, "thrust into independence and don't necessarily have the skill sets to budget their time or do time management."

That can be a background that prepares students for failure— or at least a lot of dithering around in higher education. And college performance levels seem to indicate a lack of preparedness and motivation on the part of students. Marty Nemko has seen the sad efforts of too many floundering students. As a professor at the University of Berkeley, in California, he recalls one student in a master's program who turned in solid work on papers completed outside the classroom. During the final exam, given in class, she turned in work that Nemko says could have been bettered by "the average seventh grader." Certain that she was having someone else complete her home assignments, Nemko failed her for the semester. Failing to perform in college certainly happens. One very successful college dropout interviewed for this book used to write term papers—for a hundred dollars a piece—for college students too lazy to put in the effort themselves.

Yet even for those willing to put in the time and work needed to do well at school, results don't always follow. According to the Department of Education, one-third of all undergraduates take remedial course work during their college career. And in the most recent National Assessment of Adult Literacy study, only 31 percent of college educated adults are proficient in literacy, down from 40 percent in 1992. Some of that is due to lower intelligence, but substandard performance is often the result of demoralized students.

Call a dozen educational consultants and at least a quarter will tell you that their specialty is dealing with "special-needs" children. That doesn't mean they're mentally deficient, lacking the ability to perform in the classroom or otherwise become highly productive members of society. What it means is that these people, many of them preparing to leave high school or enroll in their first years of college, have spent their lives being heavily supported by their parents and, consequently, haven't developed enough skills to function responsibly on their own. Add campus life and the sudden freedom that comes with it, and it's a formula for failure for many college freshmen. Pretty soon their lives consist of too much time at college parties, experimentation in drugs, or otherwise embracing rebellion while forgoing a career path, not to mention a way to further their education and potential career.

Ahead of the Game

In 2001, at the age of thirteen, Brian Hendricks became an entrepreneur. Building customized computers, first for friends and family and later for the community at large, he started by building one or two machines a month. Then he hit high school, befriended other computer whizzes like himself, and officially launched the company he runs today, StartUpPC.com, in Potomac, Maryland. Still living at home, Hendricks nets more than a thousand dollars a month from his company. That's not bad extra income for a seventeen-year-old when you consider that most of his peers are probably happy with monthly allowances amounting to one-tenth of that.

But the real reason Hendricks says becoming a teenage entrepreneur helped him was not about the money. It was to discover what might interest him professionally. Did he even want to be an entrepreneur forever? Would computers sustain his interest for years at a time? Did he have a talent for sales, marketing, or management? No to the first question, yes to the rest.

But the intrinsic qualities that Hendricks learned about himself were just as crucial to helping him form an idea of what to focus on next. And while he will be heading off to college this fall at the University of Michigan, he strongly suggests high school students who aren't focused on college explore entrepreneurship while in high school to better explore interests for a job down the road. Being forced to manage a staff of five and an average of fifty clients a month, Hendricks, for example, realized he's "interested in psychology and learning how to motivate people and how the brain processes tasks." He also realized he needed to work on delegating responsibilities and better managing his time. All of these lessons, he says, helped him focus not only on the business at hand, but also on what skills he might develop or cultivate for a future job.

A Set Path

Many students go "lockstep into college," says Bruce Palmer, director of admissions and marketing for the National Outdoor Leadership School (NOLS), an Outward Bound–type organization in Lander, Wyoming, that teaches outdoor leadership and survival skills to participants. In fact, Palmer, who worked as a college admissions director at Case Western University in Cleveland before joining NOLS eight years ago, says he was one of them as an undergraduate. "I could have gotten so much more out of college if I'd taken time off to figure out why I was going as opposed to just doing it," he says. "For students who have issues of keeping motivated and staying on task, I think time off can be huge."

Not every student may have the luxury of taking time off between jobs, educational choices, or transitions in life. But Brian Hendricks represents what every person without a clear picture of their career should be doing—exploring the options. That doesn't mean you have to form a business to do so. But you do have to break daily patterns and create time to assess your options.

Make the Time

Carve at least fifteen to thirty minutes out of your daily routine to consider where your interests lie, what topics are most compelling to you, and what type of daily routine you'd like your career to offer you. Start with a general picture and narrow down your options from there. Like to travel? Great. That's a general goal. Now start narrowing down fields that involve travel based upon your innate skills. If you're good with people, does a job in sales where you also need to be persuasive, or a position as tour guide where you may play a more supervisory role, sound more appealing? Both will require lots of travel, but in entirely different capacities.

Surf the Web

It's free, so why not take advantage of it? The only limit to resources online seems to be the amount of time you can dedicate to looking up information. Web sites exist not only for helping people assess their best career options, but also for writing résumés, preparing for interviews, and finding job listings specifically in your area.

Experiment Professionally

Just because it seems cool to stand up in front of a courtroom and plead someone's case doesn't make it so. Want to be a lawyer? Then start volunteering or interning in a local office. One New York high school student volunteered in the Bronx district attorney's office two years ago and realized quickly that it was a career she felt impassioned about and definitely wanted to pursue. In fact, just about every field offers internships or at least job shadowing opportunities, which can tell you not only what jobs you may like, but, as importantly, which ones you may not.

An Early Start

Of course, many Americans fritter away their young adulthood only to express regret that they didn't have the clarity at twenty to crystallize their career vision; indeed, the sentiment is endemic among workers today. But those who start careers straight out of high school likely are still ahead of the game compared with their collegiate peers—even with a failed career path or two. The driven ones, such as Chet Holmes and Brian Hendricks, feel fortunate that they experimented with different professions, despite mistakes along the way. Holmes, for example, opened a karate studio in Times Square only to see it flop. "We were starving for three years trying to make that place make money," says Holmes, who was by then married with two children. "I sold swimming pools, vacuum cleaners." And his in-laws were starting to think, "My daughter married a loser," he jokes. "Every three weeks I'm doing something completely different, making money on and off."

He wasn't a loser, of course. In fact, he was doing what many successful inventors, entrepreneurs, and successful professionals do—he was trying again and learning from his mistakes. Such failures are eye-openers and valuable lessons, according to those who launched careers early. Another woman, Dana Korey, who gave up on college after mediocre performance on several campuses in as many years, tried plenty of jobs, including event manager, movie extra supervisor, advertising sales rep, and music salesperson, before becoming an entrepreneur and starting her own business organizing people's homes and offices. Today she has dozens of clients and annual sales near seven figures.

Plowing through various jobs also builds enough resiliency to forge ahead in a different direction and eventually succeed. People who fail and try again learn to not let problems stress them out too much or become overwhelmed by adversity in their careers. In fact, they see such obstacles as opportunities— a cliché, but true. "I had the psychological profile that if someone hung up on me, I became more determined," Holmes says. It drove him to pull in eight hundred dollars a day selling pools. "You become more effective in the face of adversity."

A Different Course

But skipping the traditional educational paths doesn't mean skipping out on education. Plenty of people who launched early careers did so by enrolling in adult education courses, apprenticeships, certification programs, and positions that offered on-the-job training.

In addition, they were willing to volunteer or take entry-level positions, even if it meant just answering the phone, in fields that interested them. Doing so allows many people without college degrees to not only get the sense of a profession, but also meet other professionals within a field who could help them navigate the market to a better job. That job shadowing day where you have the chance to trail a professional whose job sounds appealing? If you're still in high school, take the opportunity. If not, try to find volunteering, mentoring, or other programs in your area that could offer a similar experience.

A host of Web sites offer a wealth of information about various educational routes that don't involve a four-year degree. They include:

◆ The American Association for Adult and Continuing Education, www.aaace.org. AAACE offers links to adult

education Web sites as well as membership meetings and
resources with offices in every state and forty countries.

♦ EducationforAdults.com, www.educationforadults.com.
This site is chock-full of listings, particularly of online
adult education programs and learning centers.

♦ Department of Labor, Employment and Training Administration, www.doleta.gov. The government's Web site
is exceedingly robust with listings for apprenticeship
programs, career centers by city, and specific programs,
including those for women and younger workers.

♦ Career Voyages, www.careervoyages.com. This site, produced by the Department of Labor, has something for just
about everybody: career changers, students struggling with
determining career paths, and parents of young adults.
The site includes listings of industries with high growth
potential, emerging industries, and tips on getting started.

Making a Move

Of course, plenty of people found success by picking up and
moving to the hottest new job market. That's a luxury not everyone can afford. But if it's something possible in your career path,
you may want to consider relocating to one of the faster-growing
areas in the country to find better job opportunities, higher salaries, and greater future job growth. Cities specifically designated
as high growth may fluctuate over time, but certain key areas
have consistently shown growth in recent years—particularly
in southern regions of the country. The US Census Bureau lists
areas of high growth on its Web site.

FASTEST-GROWING US CITIES

City	Population	Five-Year Growth	Median Household Income
Gilbert, AZ	152,025	6.6%	$78,789
Miramar, FL	101,514	6.5%	$57,172
North Las Vegas, NV	149,956	5.8%	$51,093
Henderson, NV	226,489	5.4%	$63,684
Chandler, AZ	217,811	4.5%	$65,197
Spring Valley, NV	144,618	4.4%	$51,652
Peoria, AZ	131,157	4.3%	$60,805
Joliet, IL	126,402	4.0%	$51,270
Rancho Cucamonga, CA	153,877	3.9%	$66,796
Irvine, CA	173,717	3.9%	$80,580

More than anything, experts say it's crucial to consider what it is that will keep you interested and motivated daily. Choosing a career for money, location, or growth alone may be a mistake, though these factors can play at least a secondary role in your career considerations. Listening to what others say you should do rather than listening to yourself is equally dangerous. Choosing a career is "really difficult," says Amy Barth, a career consultant and founder of Transitional Futures in Phoenixville, Pennsylvania, just outside Philadelphia. When Barth chose her first career, accounting, it was based on her parents' advice. "They said, 'Do this, because you're going to make a lot of money,'" Barth recalls. "I thought, good idea. But I came out of school and hated my job. I worked at an accounting firm in Philadelphia. I always wanted to be a social worker in high school. What I do now, helping students, is very much like social work. I'm really helping people."

Almost everyone has a career interest they've been aware of, maybe even too shy to speak of, often since early childhood. Did you fantasize as a child about becoming an actress and moving audiences with your stage performances? Why not pursue that passion? What do you have to lose? The worst thing that could happen is that you end up right back where you started. At least you gave it a shot, which is a whole lot more than most people can say about their career efforts.

It's time to pull out those old interests and reexamine them. Whether you're about to leave high school, get a GED, skip out on college, or simply change fields after more than a decade into a career, now's the time to be completely uninhibited when thinking of career goals.

Quiz: Which Career Is Best?

In today's job market, deciding on a career is no easy task, particularly when so many people switch careers—not just jobs—several times in their lives. But thinking about where your interests lie, where your skills are strongest, and a few other factors can help give you a better sense of what line of work is most suitable for you. Take the following quiz to see where your interests and abilities line up. As with the quiz at the end of chapter 1, you may want to follow up by discussing your results here with a professional career coach. But this informal exercise below can at least start you thinking about the best career plan for you.

In my ideal work environment, I'm:
  a) Working on my own.
  b) Working outside most days, moving from location to location.
  c) In an office space surrounded by other professionals.

I'm at my best:
  a) Executing a task that's handed to me.
  b) Creating my own agenda of projects.
  c) Leading a group of people.

Given the choice, I would rather:
  a) Build and assemble a tree house.
  b) Sit down and write a chapter in a novel.
  c) Organize and manage a team to clean up the city's parks.

If renovating my kitchen, I would rather:
  a) Install the appliances and cabinetry.
  b) Sketch the design of it.
  c) Oversee the renovation.

Given the choice, I would:
  a) Never leave town.
  b) Travel once a month for work.
  c) Make day trips to visit clients.

Being well paid means:
  a) Covering monthly expenses and indulging in something extravagant once a quarter.

b) Easily covering the bills and buying what I want when I want it.

c) First-class travel and five-star resorts.

My hands are best used:
   a) To build things.
   b) To write, draw, and put creative thoughts on paper.
   c) To express my thoughts through gestures while speaking.

My ideal office mate:
   a) Tells jokes, chats, and entertains me all day.
   b) Is pretty quiet and only asks me questions when she's stuck on a project we're collaborating on.
   c) Travels constantly and leaves me to work in peace alone in the office.

If I could choose, my manager would:
   a) Be very hands-on and work with me and my colleagues as a peer day in and day out.
   b) Be a resource only when needed.
   c) Offer inspiration for ideas and let me run with the execution myself.

My ideal work schedule is:
   a) Two weeks of straight work with a week off.
   b) Daily from 4 PM to 2 AM.
   c) Daily from 9 AM to 5 PM.

Tally your score and give yourself 2 points for every a) answer, 1 point for every question in which you circled b), and no points for questions you answered with c). If you scored 14 points or higher, you are well suited for trade work or work outdoors where the fruits of your labors can be appreciated at the end of each day. Such jobs include construction worker, electrician, maritime employee, police officer, and other blue-collar fields of work.

Scores ranging from 8 to 14 are reflective of those who work more independently, have a penchant for creativity and the arts, thrive best in more autonomous work situations, and like flexibility in their jobs. Fields of work would include artist, graphic designer, Web site developer, real estate agent, marketer, and other positions.

Scores below 8 reflect individuals who thrive in a more corporate environment, where they can lead others, deal with responsibility in a more structured setting, and enjoy a more executive lifestyle and the pay that accompanies it. Jobs may include everything from high-level salespeople to entrepreneurs to airline pilots.

PART II

Forging a Career Path

Chapter Three

Where to Start?

How to find the right career path is certainly the million-dollar question. But where to start is actually the most important thing to ask. Sure, you could choose a career simply by its income potential and hope you like the job—crime scene cleaners, after all, make six figures a year. But few people would have the stomach for the work. Except for those who introspectively pursue the job most inspiring to them, many enter the workforce with little thought for their careers—only to find they can't stomach whatever profession they end up in, be it accounting or garbage removal.

The good news: It's never too late to review a career and make changes—even for people well into their fifties with decades of experience under their belts. Some retirees over sixty have left corporate America after thirty years and emerged into a reinvented workplace a few years later, loving their new jobs. Still, thinking about where to begin can be dizzying: *Should I get a job directly out of high school and simply experience the work world for myself? Should I head off to college clueless about my major or professional interests? Should*

I sit at home for a year and ponder where it is I really belong? With ten years of experience behind me, should I just start searching the want ads in the hope that an appealing job will pop out at me?

Many young adults will simply follow the lead of their parents or peers, entering jobs that are accepted among their contemporaries for their status, pay, or job security, say. Often, those who have drifted in the workplace for years lack the inertia to step away from their less-than-thrilling jobs. Regardless of where you stand, there are certain crucial starting points. Doing thorough research and really examining careers through the resources below can give you a much better understanding of what the career you're thinking of pursuing entails.

The Web

You could spend a year surfing the Internet and probably not hit all the job boards it has to offer. It can be daunting enough to turn even the most diligent job enthusiast away. The good news, however, is that there are plenty of free sites available with not just job postings but advice as well—from writing that first résumé to sending the follow-up thank-you letter after an interview. Two of the best sites are listed below. A much more comprehensive list of job sites is included in appendix A. Spend a few moments checking out each of these sites and you should get a good idea of which job search tool is best suited for the type of work or field you're interested in.

◆ Quintessential Careers, www.quintcareers.com. By far, this is one of the most comprehensive job sites around for advice on everything from résumé writing to interviewing. Experts here know what they're talking about, with articles that provide practical, concrete, realistic advice for those in the market for work. The site also offers a "salary wizard" with median pay scales for dozens of professions based upon geographic areas within the country.

◆ US Department of Labor, Bureau of Labor Statistics, www.bls.gov. For those who haven't been to the government's labor Web site, the information listed on it can be daunting, to say the least. And a bear to plow through. But the site is well organized and lists detailed reports of jobs, salaries, and occupations that are expected to grow—even how those jobs are projected to grow within each state. Go to www.projectionscentral.com to check out long- and short-term job growth projections in any state. The best offering from the Department of Labor, however, is the annual *Occupational Outlook Handbook*—perhaps the job seeker's bible for specific job titles—which can be purchased at bookstores or perused at your local library. The book contains detailed descriptions of hundreds of jobs, their salary outlook, and the nature of the work, in addition to the growth potential in the coming decade for each of those jobs. In addition, check out the Department of Labor's magazine *Occupational Outlook Quarterly* (*OOQ*), which can be found online at www.bls.gov/opub/ooq/ooqhome.htm. It's much more user-friendly than the intensive research statistics on the organization's main page, and includes a fun, highly informative section called "Grab Bag" that contains articles about various jobs, tips, and career advice.

School Counselors

If you're still in school, taking a class at a community college, or otherwise able to access guidance counselors or career center workers, they're great resources for investigating what type of job may be most suitable for your skills and interests. These people are trained to help would-be careerists such as yourself get on the right path to a fulfilling career. Dozens of career assessment tests are available online as well, but most of them cost money, and the validity of results generated by answering a few questions you type into a computer can be dubious compared with one-on-one counseling with professionals who have spent their careers studying the job market and various ways of entering it.

Informational Interviews

Talk to those who have gone before you. It's an old tactic—and one shunned by many employers after years of eager young job seekers tried to land jobs under the guise of an "informational interview." But talking to the very people who are involved in a career you may want to pursue is one of the best ways to get a true sense of what that career is like. Particularly when you're not interviewing for a specific position, professionals are often willing to be very open about the pros and cons of an industry, position, and even the particular company they may be working for. You can try the old-fashioned way of picking up the phone and hoping you get willing participants on the other end who would welcome a visit to their office to shed light on what it is they do day in and day out. That certainly happens on occasion. But you might find better luck by attending a trade association meeting in your area where you can meet people within that industry. No such meetings? Try your local community college or union, where teachers and representatives for the field could either tell you more about it—or point you to someone who could.

Job Fairs

Sort of like speed dating, but for jobs, these fairs offer those exploring a certain job market the opportunity to see what types of positions are available in their field, as well as giving company recruiters access to hundreds of potential job candidates. And who knows? Even though you're just investigating, you may end up landing an internship or even a job by talking to and impressing a recruiter. They're not just for college grads anymore. No matter your age, job fairs are open to anyone and are sometimes targeted for specific industries and geographic areas. Online job boards, such as CareerBuilder, sponsor job fairs throughout the country, listing the location and date of each one on their Web site. Check job boards for such events. Also, ask local chapters of national associations if they conduct any job fairs, as well as local colleges—just because you don't attend doesn't mean you can't get invited to the recruitment festivities.

Friends and Family

As I've noted previously, friends and family are resources to use carefully. Still, they can offer some insight into your career. Depending on how much you trust and value the opinions of those you surround yourself with every day, your friends, family, and peers may be the first or last stop on your career search travels, but they should definitely not be neglected. The key, of course, is to seek out information from those whose opinions and advice you trust. Your best friend who thinks you can do no wrong is probably not a good place to start—she won't offer much objectivity. Siblings, parents, or friends who know your strengths and weaknesses well, and aren't afraid to have a frank discussion with you about them, are a great sounding board and testing place to run your career ideas through. They may also reveal some aspects of your personality or skill sets that you hadn't thought of—but they're keenly aware of after knowing you for years.

A Fuzzy Future

As Josh Flowerman finished his senior year of high school in 1997, he wasn't exactly burning up the academic charts. "I was an average student," he says, though he was accepted at a few big-name schools. Then reality hit. "My parents asked me what I wanted to study. I said, 'I don't know. I'll figure it out when I get to college.'" That's when his parents slammed on the brakes. "They said, 'Hold on,'" Flowerman recalls of his parents' alarm at this lack of career focus. Rather than plunk twenty thousand or more dollars into a fruitless freshman year, Flowerman's parents suggested he take time to figure out what it was he really wanted to study.

Kudos to these parents for putting a halt to a potentially unfocused, futile college experience. But exactly how to take time off and ponder the best move wasn't clear at first—to Flowerman or his parents. Should he simply hang out and think about his options? Was getting a job in town the best way to consider his future career? Should he hole up with advisers and aptitude tests to unearth hidden talents that might unlock a professional gateway to happiness and riches?

Flowerman decided to do none of the above. Instead, he enrolled in a program called Dynamy. The organization, started in 1969, was tailor-made for people like Flowerman—smart, energetic, and seemingly college-bound high school students who simply have no idea what career to embark on. Rather than waste money at a four-year university figuring out that very question, programs like Dynamy's take students for a semester or year at a time, helping them to form leadership skills and greater responsibility for their career choices. The Worcester, Massachusetts–based organization, with programs in Worcester and Santa Rosa, California, offers more than two hundred types of internships for enrollees, from glassblowing to reporting.

Flowerman, who had always been obsessed with sports, signed on to work for the Holy Cross College Athletic Department. To get his feet wet, he performed basic administrative duties—filing and copying papers. Then he suggested he could do far more. The school gave him an opportunity by allowing him to write articles for the school's magazine.

In another internship for the Worcester Icecats, a team within the American Hockey League (it has since moved to Peoria, Illinois), Flowerman went to every game and wrote press releases for the organization. "These internships definitely helped guide me to the first phase of my career," Flowerman says. Ironically, that involved joining his brother, who founded Career Explorations, an internship program similar to Dynamy's but oriented toward students still in high school. The program, started in 2003, offers high school students the opportunity to come to New York and participate in virtually any internship of their choice. Its goal is to provide mentors to those who may be in the throes of trying to figure out the right career path. With sixteen students the first year, the program has grown to include ninety-one as of this writing, with fifty-six in New York and the remainder in a new program to start in Boston. Career Explorations participants have had some amazing experiences, including:

- Designing a pair of Bill Blass jeans.
- Promoting soccer games for the New York MetroStars (now known as the Red Bulls).
- Campaigning for Congressman Anthony Weiner when he ran against New York's Mayor Michael Bloomberg.
- Critiquing movie scripts.
- X-raying animals at a veterinary hospital.

The point is to help participants get a jump start on their careers by briefly immersing them in their areas of interest. "The idea is that somebody who is really focused can find out whether this is something they want to pursue as a career or a course of study," Flowerman says. "But alternatively, it's equally as important that they figure out if this is what they *do not* want to do."

Indeed, taking a year and a hard look at your career in a structured environment is probably one of the most important and productive things you can do. And there are plenty of organizations to help you find your way. The key is not to feel as though putting all your eggs in one program or experience, so to speak, is going to reveal the right career for you. Many people participate in internships, apprenticeships, certification programs, and classes only to realize that what they're doing is not at all what they imagined the field to be like. That's actually a good thing, experts say. Better to find out what turns you off now, through an internship, than on day four of a job to which you've already made a yearlong commitment.

Mind the Gap

Many career advisers suggest taking time off from school or the workplace to really assess your next best career move and figure out what line of work is best suited for your skills and interests. In a survey conducted at one Philadelphia high school by Transitional Futures, nearly 250 students were asked if they had been using their guidance counselor's office to obtain career advice. Only 23 percent said yes—and of those, only half were certain of their career path. "I found that pretty surprising," says Amy Barth, an organizer of the survey. In an accompanying focus group across all grades within that same school, students reported that their parents were the biggest influence in their lives. That held true for career choices as well. Yet widely accepted "research says that parents feel it's the responsibility of schools and counselors to provide career-related advice," according to Barth.

Where does that leave students? Often falling through the cracks, say some educational experts. Too many high school students are pushed into the nation's universities because they and their families assume that's where they belong. But without a clear vision for where they're headed, students are simply lost on college campuses—at least academically, and ultimately in their careers as well.

In fact, when the nationally recognized college testing service ACT recently surveyed middle and high school students, it found that almost a quarter of eighth and ninth graders had given no thought to their post-high-school plans. Shouldn't kids be allowed to be kids? many would ask. And the answer is yes. But with little thought to what lies ahead after high school graduation, many seniors will no doubt get shuffled into the nation's universities, and waste time and money spinning their wheels in classes that don't pertain to the profession they'll ultimately choose.

But Barth brings up an issue that muddies the career plans of students even further: Most middle and high schools expose students to traditional careers, whether they're blue or white collar. Unique jobs that might be more inspiring—curator, deep-sea diver, biological weapons specialist (an area of expertise likely to be of high demand in the years ahead)—are rarely, if ever, presented. "In general, high school kids don't know what they want to do," Barth says. "In workshops, some say they want to be an electrical engineer. You ask them, 'Why do you want to do that?' They don't have a reason. Or, 'Why do you want to be a lawyer?' 'Well, you make a lot of money.' "

Neither of those answers will sustain a fulfilling career. In the school where Barth works, the counselor-to-student ratio averages one counselor for every twelve hundred students. So most of a counselor's time is spent arranging class schedules, not conducting meaningful, one-on-one career counseling sessions.

That leaves those in search of a career choice either passively moving through their adult years in search of one, or grabbing at other experts who can help them out. When that happens, some people—young and old alike—turn to educational consultants or career coaches. Educational consultants, intimately familiar with college admissions processes and even individual campuses and their surrounding areas, can also help guide students trying to avoid the collegiate market. But for high school students uninterested in college, these consultants can charge a pretty penny to tell you what you already know—college isn't right for you. Still, they, as well as career coaches, can help both young and older individuals who are wondering about their careers to at least narrow down their focus to a few key areas. Another option is to explore free or inexpensive career advice in your area—often available at community colleges or adult learning centers. The key: Explore as many low-cost options as you can. The more you know, the better the career decision you can make.

A Year Off

The lack of focus and responsibility developed under too lenient parents or an education system that let them slip through the cracks suggests that many students would be far better off by doing what many young adults in foreign countries have been doing for years—taking a gap year off to figure out where their professional strengths and interests lie. In England, for example, it's practically standard practice these days. And for good reason.

Countries such as England have long encouraged young adults to take a year off, or a "gap year" as it's called, to really think about what type of school, profession, or direction they would like to take. Over decades that idea has been gaining momentum in the United States as well, albeit slowly. At least a third of all students who enter the National Outdoor Leadership School, for example, do so because they aren't certain what career or college they would like to pursue, according to the organization's Bruce Palmer.

Gap-year programs such as NOLS effectively narrow a participant's career focus and sense of purpose. "I have the impression that some of our graduates might have continued to flop around" had they not entered a gap-year program, says Jim Zuberbuhler, who heads the similar Dynamy program. "Others might have become accountants when they should be social workers."

That, too, is the point of many programs—to encourage participants to be more honest with themselves about their true career interests, even if it means saying good-bye to their fantasy of becoming a three-hundred-grand-a-year cardiothoracic surgeon. An ideal job for some, certainly. But for those who hate math or the thought of twelve years of schooling, it's time to put that dream to rest.

For people who participate in gap-year programs, it can mean travel abroad, hard labor building homes in impoverished neighborhoods, or jumping feetfirst into an accounting internship. Plenty of programs exist. At NOLS, for example, a gap year means embarking on outdoor programs that teach leadership skills in places like Patagonia, New Zealand, Australia, Wyoming, Arizona, and the Pacific Northwest. Groups of participants must rely on one another and on their organizational skills to complete these arduous programs, designed to create confidence, leadership, motivation, and greater focus in participants.

Palmer, who was formerly a college admissions director, is convinced that a straight path to college isn't always the most strategic route. "I was someone who lockstepped and did what I was supposed to do. I could have gotten so much more out of college if I had taken time off to figure out why it is I was going as opposed to just doing it," he admits. "For students who have motivational and staying-on-task issues, I think time off can be huge. It is a big jump from high school into the college ranks."

The majority of NOLS graduates do end up finishing college, Palmer says—but many change their majors upon returning to school. And those who don't finish college, he adds, often go on to establish careers with the much greater sense of purpose developed by living in an unsettling wilderness where maturity and responsibility are the keys to survival.

Similar programs offer everything from wilderness hikes to urban work experiences, and though they can cost as much as twenty thousand dollars a year, many offer scholarships or financial assistance for those who qualify but can't afford the tuition.

If you're considering an outdoor-based program, make sure you love the great outdoors—or are willing to adapt to it. Many programs involve wilderness treks in which participants work in groups for days on end, making hiking plans, preparing food, setting up camp, and completing other activities that require relying on others for survival—an outdoor equivalent of office teamwork. Others focus more on community building projects in various parts of the world. All are geared to give participants an adventure and experiences unavailable through traditional education or work paths. So focused are programs, says Zuberbuhler, that even though the majority of participants continue on to college, "a growing number, particularly in technology, choose to go directly into the workforce."

Gap-Year Programs

- ◆ Dynamy, www.dynamy.org. One of the nation's oldest experiential educational groups, Dynamy was founded in 1969. It targets students just exiting high school and those who have decided to take a year off after some course work at college. Students live in group apartments and share household duties. Programs are available on both the East and West Coasts. The program, which offers two hundred intern categories at any given time, is so popular that the organization receives some twelve hundred inquiries for the sixty-five spots open to participants yearly. That's up from six hundred inquiries a few years ago. *Cost:* $23,000. Some financial aid is available.

◆ National Outdoor Leadership School (NOLS), www. nols .edu. Founded in 1965, NOLS was formed to foster leadership skills and has seen more than seventy-five thousand participants since then. The organization offers programs in Patagonia, New Zealand, Australia, India, Alaska, the western United States, Mexico, and on Baffin Island in the Canadian Arctic. Courses cover everything from mountaineering to wilderness medicine. *Cost:* Tuition varies, but ranges from $8,000 to $11,000 per semester. More than $800,000 a year is available in scholarships.

◆ Outward Bound, www.outwardboundwilderness.org. One of the most popular and best-known adventure programs in the country, Outward Bound offers programs for both individuals and corporations, for people of any age. Participants engage in both solo and group activities that build wilderness, team, and leadership skills, often over the course of a week or so. *Cost:* From $700 to $6,000 for semester programs. More than $2 million in scholarships are given each year.

◆ Bridge Year, www.bridgeyear.com. This program is geared toward recent high school graduates who are uncertain about what to study in college or if college is even the right choice for them. It places students into gap-year programs in Chile and Argentina, where participants experience outdoor activities and heavy Spanish-language immersion courses. *Cost:* $6,775 to $13,305.

◆ The Center for Interim Programs, www.interimprograms .com. This organization, launched in 1980, helps individuals find the right gap-year program for them. It features information on programs for kids (working with Mexican street children), social services (building houses for the impoverished), the arts (glassblowing), specific skills training (guitar building), and dozens of other activities. *Cost:* $2,100.

Apprenticeships

For a trade worker, an apprenticeship is often not only the best way to learn trade skills that meet the most stringent union standards, but actually the gateway into various jobs as well. In an apprenticeship, people interested in trade work learn valuable skills while getting paid to do so. Still, don't assume that skipping college to pursue an apprenticeship means you won't be studying and learning for years on end.

Apprenticeships, of which there are more than 850 nationally, last from one to six years, and are generally open to people eighteen and older, though in some cases people as young as sixteen can qualify. The Department of Labor Web site lists dozens of apprenticeship programs throughout the country: www.doleta.gov/atels_bat/fndprgm.cfm. While enrolled in an apprenticeship, wages generally start at half those of an experienced journey-level worker, but rise to hourly wages equal to that of those with a bachelor's or even master's degrees, depending on the skill levels learned.

Vocational Schools

The beauty of vocational schools is that they can offer you a chance to learn about various industries, whether or not you might develop or enjoy the skills needed to work in them, but with a much more modest commitment of time and money than a four-year program would require.

Want to be a makeup artist, but your "makeovers" leave your subjects looking clownish? Better to find that out now in an initial class than to embark on a career for which your skills simply aren't a match.

Sadly, however, some vocational schools are little more than shams—diploma mills looking to make a quick buck. Consider the following tips from the Federal Trade Commission before choosing a school:

- ◆ Determine if vocational training is even necessary. Many positions offer on-the-job training where you can get paid to learn the same skills.
- ◆ Compare the curricula among competing programs. Are the courses the same? Do they offer similar skill sets?
- ◆ Audit a course. The best way to tell if an instructor is worth his or her salt and to see how much individual attention is given to each student is to sit in on a course. If an instructor balks at this, that's a sign to walk away.

- Ask for a list of program graduates who can give feedback about the school's educational value. Then ask those students for referrals to other people—after all, the school will most likely send you off to talk to straight-A students who are likely to give glowing reviews.
- Ask if materials, such as books and uniforms, are included in the cost of the program. Better programs are usually less likely to nickel-and-dime students.
- Make sure the school is accredited—and don't just take the school's word for it. Ask for the name and number of its accrediting group. Then call that number and verify the accreditation.
- Check to make sure there aren't inordinate numbers of complaints against the school lodged with the Better Business Bureau.
- Check the Department of Education's searchable database of accredited schools nationwide: http://ope.ed .gov/accreditation/.

Certifications

When Kristin Crockett, the human resources benefits manager for Qwest, presents her résumé for a new job or position, she has no reservations about the fact that it doesn't include a college degree. Fifteen years of experience and certificates in various human resources specialties back up her skills, she says. Crockett's six certifications include everything from customer service to diversity training.

For certain fields, such as health care and information technology, certifications can actually be more valued than a college degree. "People get four-year degrees and spend a couple of years in the workplace where nothing's happening. Then they come back to the junior college to get certified in a blue-collar job," says Impact Publications' Ron Krannich, when they realize "they can make sixty thousand dollars a year as an electrician."

The point Krannich so aptly makes is that for many professions, certifications are a far faster, easier, more appropriate way to a job than a bachelor's degree. How to find a certification program right for the skills you need? You might begin by checking with the association for your industry. A simple Web search using Google or another search engine should pull up various industry organizations. Many offer continuing education and certification programs—or links to centers that do.

Then get a list of the classes and certificate programs offered at your local community college. Community and junior colleges offer certifications that can range from fire inspector to Web designer. Such certifications are a great way to not only gain valuable skills and information about a particular field, but also increase your stature against other candidates when applying for jobs.

Internships

Internships have long been an invaluable way to get work experience without committing completely to a particular field. Even better news: Unlike years past, when internships were essentially an acceptable form of slavery, today most companies pay their interns, offering hourly rates far above minimum wage. Internships are an ideal way to enter fields that are particularly hard to break into. And for interns with initiative and drive, impressing a supervisor on an internship can often lead to full-time work.

If you're currently attending college but thinking of leaving, you might want to check out any internship listings your academic department has listed within its offices before you walk off the campus never to return. If you've already done that, there are still plenty of resources available for those who want to pursue an internship. A few of them are listed here:

- ◆ Corporate Internships, www.corporateinterns.com. People within college as well as those who are not can register with this company which places candidates in various paid corporate internships throughout the year. Fields include business, communications, engineering, and information technology. *Cost:* Free.
- ◆ Career Explorations, www.ceinternships.com. Career Explorations offers high school students monthlong internships at companies in New York and Boston. The program is ideal for students with far-reaching aspirations, since program organizers will find an internship for just about any profession imaginable. One recent example? Aerial photography. *Cost:* $5,395. This fee includes room and board, activities outside the internship, and all meals except lunch.
- ◆ Summer Search, www.summersearch.org. Summer Search, started in 1990 and based in San Francisco, offers low-income teenagers scholarships to participate in internships, experiential education programs, mentoring, and professional development courses. The program serves approximately six hundred students a year. *Cost:* Free to students who qualify.

♦ Julian Krinsky Camps & Programs, www.jkcp.com. Founded in 1978 by former professional tennis player Julian Krinsky, the Philadelphia-based program offers a rich array of programs for high school students from sports activities to professional internships, including a program at the Wharton School of Business for high school seniors who qualify. *Cost:* $3,750 to $8,750.

♦ Student Government Jobs, www.studentjobs.gov. A joint project between the US Office of Personnel Management and the Department of Education, Student Government Jobs isn't so much about internships or gap-year positions as it is about helping students find work in the government sector, much of it short-lived and seasonal. This provides students a chance to get their feet wet in positions without making a permanent commitment. Jobs usually last a summer, ranging from park guide to aircraft mechanic, and are listed by state. Many positions pay upward of eleven dollars an hour. *Cost:* Free.

Temporary Jobs

The name alone—*temporary*—doesn't sound too promising when it comes to career opportunities. But temporary positions are, without a doubt, one of the best and fastest ways to full-time work. And as a job search tool, the usefulness of temp work is only likely to improve, if you look at Bureau of Labor statistics. In 2005, 2.5 million wage and salary jobs were provided through temporary firms. That's an 8.7 percent increase from 2004, according to the American Staffing Association (ASA).

The beauty of temporary work, of course, is that you can always walk away if a job is unappealing. On the other hand, getting into an office, particularly in a field that may spark your interest, gives you a sense of what it's like to work for a company in that particular profession and what types of jobs you may be suited for. In fact, many agencies specialize in not just temporary work but temporary to permanent and permanent placement.

Even if you're only seeking out temporary and not full-time work, working as a temp allows you to meet people within that profession, ask questions about certain positions, and, if you work hard enough, impress those you work with to help you seek out positions within that firm or elsewhere within the industry.

Trying to decide which temporary firm to work for? Many offer basically the same services, competitive pay, and even benefits (if you put in enough hours). Really, the important decision about a temp agency is which one is most likely to give you the best chance of getting experience in your particular field of interest. Not sure what you're interested in? Then you've got nothing to lose. You can always leave one temp agency for another—although it's advisable to complete your current assignment before doing so, since the next firm will ask you for references from previous employers.

The best way to find a firm? If you've got the time, you could contact several of the companies in your area that you might be interested in working with, asking them what staffing firm they use. Or you can search for temporary agencies by zip code, industry interest, and type of position on the ASA Web site. Visit www.americanstaffing.net/jobseekers/find_company.cfm.

A final thought about starting your job search: You want to find the best job for you, not the best job, period. In other words, be realistic. The absolutely perfect job doesn't exist. Every profession has its pluses and minuses. Even movie stars who make millions and bask in the glow of the adoring public hate the way they're forced to relinquish personal privacy to stalking paparazzi. The key to finding the ideal job is loving most of what the job entails—responsibilities, pay, co-workers, environment, freedom, or whatever aspect of the work you find unbeatable.

Chapter Four

Jobs with Freedom

When Brent Hodgins started his branding consultancy a few years ago, he did so with a goal firmly in mind: "To build a highly profitable business that supports the life that each of us wants to build," he says of himself and his staff. Sounds like a great starting point.

This goal is reflective of many people's intent these days to find jobs that not only inspire them but liberate them as well—be it in the work's requirements, hours, pay, flexibility, or other rewards. For all today's professionals—with degrees and without—balancing work and life is crucial to career happiness. The good news is that those without four-year degrees aren't at all beholden to slave-wage jobs that require adhering to a tight schedule or punching in on the company clock. At Hodgins's branding consultancy, Mirren Business Development, in New York, Hodgins and his staff plan to build their company as much around their life outside of work as they do around the needs of their clients. Next summer Hodgins's goal is to move the company to Whistler, British Columbia, for three months. In the winter, the company, tucked into the bottom

floor of a brownstone in the East Village, might spend a week
on Vermont's slopes while working in between ski runs.

Such a transient company may be an anomaly, but Hodgins,
who began his career by walking away from college soon after
he started, learned early on that rewarding jobs not only can be
had without a college degree but can be particularly robust in
the level of freedom they offer as well.

He actually learned this lesson by accident—or rather, by
necessity. Hodgins, who grew up on a dairy farm an hour outside Vancouver, started his "career" by striking at the age of five
to push for a raise on his five-cents-a-month salary. "Fortunately,
my parents thought it was hilarious," he says.

He knew they wouldn't think the same of the twelve hundred
dollars in parking tickets he accrued in his freshman year while at
the University of British Columbia in Vancouver. "On my birth-
day, my ticket arrives and I'm a broke college student with twelve
hundred bucks in bills in my hands," Hodgins says. "I proceed to
freak out." Mostly because not paying the fine meant a suspended
license. Telling his parents was certainly not an option. Solution?
Hodgins decided to throw a party. A four-dollar-a-head, hundreds-
strong, DJ-driven, blowout college party. To do so, Hodgins enlisted
three of the most popular students on campus and asked them to
spread the word. Hodgins pulled in enough to pay his tickets and
put a little away besides. "I was like, *I think there's an opportunity
here*. So a couple of months later, I did it again." The outcome?
"I packed the place again," he says. The partners with popularity
whom he had initially enlisted to draw in the crowds grew tired of
their role, so Hodgins took on the parties entirely on his own.

He threw more parties. And made more money. By the time
the events grew to three-thousand-person affairs and required
renting out the air hangar at Vancouver International Airport, it

dawned on Hodgins that he was finding much more success and inspiration outside college than he was in the lecture hall. And having a blast doing it.

That's when Hodgins left the campus and focused more on throwing parties, forming partnerships with local TV and radio stations, and building an increasing reputation for his fetes, which cleared upward of sixty thousand dollars a night.

Throwing those parties "consumed a lot of my time," Hodgins recalls. But they gave him freedom in the sense that he was now his own boss, even if it was short-lived. Over the next six years, he built his party business to such a size that it attracted the attention of a national event planner moving its business into Vancouver. Hodgins, sensing he was outclassed in size (Hodgins's company threw two hundred parties a year, while the competitor topped out around a thousand), approached the firm's CEO with an offer. "I convinced him, with knees shaking under the table, that the only way into the market was through me," Hodgins relates, now laughing at his unwarranted arrogance. But he did have one thing on his side: "I had the contract locked up with the biggest radio market in the area," he says. "So we brokered a deal."

Indeed he did. Hodgins ended up selling his business that day, but the notion that he could have that much freedom professionally—to run his own company, make decisions about when to work, broker a deal to sell the firm—was an appealing idea that he carried forth in subsequent jobs.

The Value of Freedom

A job that offers freedom—who wouldn't want that? To some it may sound crazy, but not everyone finds jobs with immense freedom appealing. If you prefer structured hours, a more controlled workplace, or a more process-oriented professional experience—and those jobs can have their benefits—it's important to admit that to yourself now. But for people who enjoy working odd hours, having two weeks off at a stretch, being asked to travel on the fly, and being on call at a moment's notice, such jobs can be both demanding and rewarding—and many don't require a college degree.

If you think jobs with freedom only come when you've reached the top of corporate America after years of formal education and grinding work, well, some of them do. But plenty don't. And if you're reconsidering your career without a degree—and, obviously you are, or you wouldn't be reading this book—now is the time to completely free yourself in not only the career choice you ultimately make, but how you go about getting there as well.

Setting Yourself Free

Remember, even the most liberating jobs can still be constricting at times. The point is to clarify your definition of *freedom*. What does freedom mean to you? Does it mean:

- ◆ Making your own schedule?
- ◆ Making more money to have spending power and freedom outside of work?
- ◆ Balancing your life and work perfectly?
- ◆ Being able to call your own shots at work and dictate what projects are assigned to you?
- ◆ Working part of the year and having part of the year off?

◆ Being able to telecommute?

◆ Working alone?

Twelve Jobs with Freedom

Every job has some restrictions, but some offer far fewer than others; you can set your own hours, dictate your pay, even choose with whom and where you work. Here's a list of some of the more liberating occupations.

Job	Why It's Liberating	Potential Yearly Income
Pilot	Travel the globe on an airline's dime.	$100,000+
Maritime worker	Same as above, except on a ship, with weeks off at a time.	$80,000
Oil rig worker	Vast amounts of time off; hours alone to sit and think or read (don't knock it till you try it).	$100,000
House inspector	Set your own hours.	$80,000
Real estate investor	Live off your purchases.	$100,000+
Freelance journalist	Choose what *you* want to write about.	$100,00+
Consultant	Name your own hours.	$100,000+
Police officer	Frequent movement.	$75,000
Dog walker	Set your own hours.	$60,000
Personal chef	Create your own menu.	$100,000+
Boat captain	Travel on swanky yachts.	$150,000
Salesperson	Be in control of your income; work on your own.	$100,000+

If the idea of one of the jobs above sounds appealing, then you're not alone. But how to get there? Let's explore a few of these careers in greater depth, as well as ways to go about landing them.

Dog Days of Employment

If you love animals almost as much as making your own work schedule, then becoming a dog walker may be the perfect job. You simply show up, take Fido for a walk, and then drop him off happy again at his home, right? Well, sort of. Dog walking and sitting services have been popular for years in cities like New York, where walkers have been known to jaunt along sidewalks with up to half a dozen pooches at a time tied to leads. But in recent years, the industry has been moving beyond big cities to virtually everywhere in the country. And for good reason. These days, the pet industry is a thirty-six-billion-dollar-a-year market. Americans love their pets, and they're willing to pay almost anything to make them happy—shelling out big bucks every year for pet food, clothing, toys, treats, and animal care services.

That's good news for people looking to get into the industry. In fact, *Entrepreneur* magazine names dog walking and sitting services as one of the ten best pet businesses to start. It's easy to see why. It costs virtually nothing to launch a dog walking business. Have a hundred dollars in your pocket? Then you're well on your way. All that's needed are a few supplies like extra leashes and dog treats as well as a few posters offering your services to post in neighborhoods and office buildings. It's relatively easy to build up a client base of a few dozen dogs or more within the first six months to a year of launching your business.

One dog walker in New York is so busy, she's been forced to hire extra walkers to help her out.

Getting Started

Flyers are certainly a way to let others know about your services. But there are additional paths to this occupation, and some even involve getting paid. When one New York dog walker started her business several years ago, she did so after working as a pet caretaker at Biscuits and Bath, a New York day care center for dogs, essentially, that offers daily dog sitting, bathing services, and supplies. Not only was she getting paid to take care of animals—something she loved—but she was learning about the business of pet care in the process. And because she was observing other dog walkers in her daily routine, she was able to get a good sense of the pay potential (sixty to seventy thousand dollars a year or more) as well as entrepreneurial aspects of being a dog walker, such as subcontracting out other dog walkers as business expands.

Today she has dozens of clients she walks dogs for daily and house sits for on weekends and holidays. She loves dogs, which is why most people get into this line of work. But it can have its downfalls, particularly in a city like New York. If it's twenty degrees out and snowing with a foot of drifts still to come down, for instance, you may feel like staying inside and curling up under a blanket with a good book. Unfortunately, Fido's bladder is still calling. And somebody's got to let him out. One city dog walker recalled how he prepared for work each day in the winter by dressing in three layers of socks, three layers of pants, and four shirts, topped by a hooded sweatshirt and coat before heading outdoors. In addition to protecting your own body, many dogs, smaller breeds in particular, also need protective gear before they head outdoors. For dogs not keen on the idea of wearing snow booties to protect their paws from salt on the roads, putting on such items can be a time-consuming struggle and extreme job frustration for walkers. Fluffy's bladder may be about to burst, but she doesn't realize that relieving that tension means strapping on those Velcro booties in order to go outside. And she's happy to spend another hour in her home fighting the dog walker tooth and nail to avoid those irritating little paw covers.

Another consideration: Dogs are sweet, but they're not sophisticated. And their moods can swing like an erratic pendulum. That can mean an easily manageable dog one day becomes a terror the next. Many owners, enamored of their pup's warm daily welcome and wagging tail, think just greeting them at the door every day is obedience enough. Their unruly dogs can be your work hazard. You'll need to know how to deal with temperament issues at any moment.

Finally, the business is fraught with client turnover. People move, dogs die. Sounds harsh, but it's true. Over time, there are plenty of reasons why your services will no longer be needed. If you are only comfortable in a business where you can lock in a certain percentage of clients for years on end, then this might not be the job for you.

On the other hand, there are plenty of perks to be had in the dog walking industry, starting with the animals themselves. Yes, they can be temperamental. They're also amazingly warm, sweet, charming little creatures with cheerful personalities. A multitude of studies have shown the stress-relieving value of working with animals—from lengthening life expectancies to helping people recover from major surgery. Being around creatures this life sustaining can only be good for your health, and your job satisfaction.

And don't forget that while the dogs are walking, so are you. Plenty of dog walkers vouch for the exercise running such a business offers them, often losing weight in the process. Not many jobs pay you while you shed pounds!

A final upside: You can generally get time off when you need it. You have to be reliable and available when clients are out of town. And you may need to give up a weekend here or there to house sit your top client's pooch. On the other hand, being your own boss means you can take days off here and there when need be.

Facts on Fido

My Pet Business offers the following pet industry info:

- Pet care is one of the fastest-growing industries in the country today.
- In America, forty million households have at least one dog.
- In households that have pets, 47 percent have more than one.
- Some thirty-five billion dollars is spent on pet products each year.

Getting Lassie on a Leash

Just because you had a family dog growing up doesn't mean you're an expert at caring for someone else's. Customers will be trusting their beloved animals to your care, so you'd better know what you're doing. The best way to find out may be to volunteer your time at an animal shelter, veterinary office, or dog day care facility. It will give you a firsthand look at what's required in animal care as well as the most effective ways to train and control our furry little friends.

Sources of Information

Check out My Pet Business, www.mypetbusiness.com. This site offers tips on how to become a dog walker as well as a series of instructional videotapes to get your business started. Take a look as well at the National Association of Professional Pet Sitters Web site, www.petsitters.org, which offers a smattering of information for those looking to get into the business.

Restaurants to Real Estate

For years, Glenn Mazzone bounced from one restaurant job to another, making good money as he took orders from customers at Greek, Mexican, and Spanish establishments, and even an old train station converted to a restaurant. "I did it for twenty-four years and eleven months," Mazzone says. "I worked at every restaurant you can imagine. I like to move around a lot." And working in the food and beverage industry certainly provides that opportunity—with salaries near low six figures for those in high-end establishments. In fact, plenty of people who get into the restaurant business do so because they find it liberating—offering quick cash, flexible hours, and the opportunity to take those skills and move to different cities or even countries, and easily find work again. One woman who made a career of restaurant work did so not because she loved serving platefuls of food to hungry customers. She worked for six months at a stretch, saved the plentiful cash she picked up from tips, then took off for another several months and traveled the world. Anytime she was running low on money, she simply picked up another job as a server.

Mazzone, who has never married or had children, loved the feeling of always being mobile, always free to hop from one fine-dining restaurant to the next, knowing a healthy income would be there waiting for him. "I lived literally all over California." But then one day he'd had enough. "The first five to ten years waiting tables is very social and you always have money at hand. But you can't do that for the rest of your life," Mazzone says. "I saw older waiters telling stories and how beat they looked." He didn't want to become one of them. So Mazzone started crafting a plan to move on. By November 2005, he was out.

Never one with a penchant for college, Mazzone instead spent his life educating himself. Finding a new career path was no different. With a former boyfriend, who showed him the value of real estate ownership, Mazzone developed the idea of buying and flipping houses. He had purchased his first home more than a decade ago, while still waiting tables, for ten thousand dollars. In subsequent years, he purchased an additional eleven properties, reselling most of them. The most recent homes he bought are like the one in Dana Point, California, which he purchased for $680,000 in 2002 and sold two years later for $975,000. In another instance, he purchased a unit within a building for $140,000 and flipped it for $345,000.

Over time, he's learned some valuable lessons: Buy at least 10 percent under market value, make sure you're willing to live in it if need be, and don't rush to sell too early. But the best lesson has been one of freedom. Mazzone, who now lives in Florida but holds a real estate license in California, is also looking at property in New Mexico and the Midwest. Making low six figures turning over houses allows him to hop around the country when the best property becomes available, and dictate his own living style and environment. "I want more control where I live," Mazzone says, happy with his ability to redesign an apartment or house to his liking, or choosing the location that suits him and his business plan best. "I don't want to be subjected to the whims of some landlord because he wants to kick me out."

Owning his own property has indeed meant massive freedom for Mazzone. Part of that comes with being an entrepreneur and making his own decisions (an idea further explored in chapter 5). But it also comes with answering to no one but himself—a wonderful feeling for Mazzone after years of rotating through scheduled restaurant shifts. For people who flip houses, the job requires no set hours, no meetings with marketing staffs, their own choice of location in which to live, and plenty of time off if they choose. But that doesn't mean it's simply a matter of buying a home and selling it three months later. Television shows like *Flip This House* make the process look so easy. In reality, you have to know what you're doing—and that means understanding the housing market, legal requirements, construction costs, and property values.

The Freedom That Housing Built

The key, of course, is buying and reselling a home that will make a nice profit. Flipping houses certainly has its risks, but the rewards can be immense for those who are successful. The key, of course, is knowing how to gauge a good buy. A fixer-upper is what you're looking for. But you want to make sure the run-down house you turn around is going to be appealing for its location as much as its face-lift. Mazzone suggests buying the worst house in the best neighborhood.

Also, learn to spot gentrification. The ideal buy is one ahead of the curve in an area that's about to be developed. If you see a few homes refinished and a few high-end cafés going up in a particular neighborhood, those are likely strong signs of a gentrifying area. "The smallest house in a cool little pocket neighborhood" that's just starting to come to life can mean a house that doubles in value from when you buy it to the time you sell it, according to Mazzone.

Finally, skip the hard labor. Mazzone is fairly handy, so he's able to complete some of the repair jobs his homes need on his own. But unless you have a strong house-flipping business and are well versed and loaded with contacts in the world of housing renovation, you will probably only create more hassle and hurdles for yourself as you fix the place up. Ideally, the best homes to buy are those that only need cosmetic changes. A home that can be transformed through painting, switching out cabinetry, replacing plumbing fixtures, and other simple changes is the best—and cheapest—to flip.

Getting Started

For detailed information and expert advice on flipping houses, check out the following resources:

◆ *Renovate to Riches: Buy, Improve, and Flip Houses to Create Wealth.* This guide offers general information for those looking to get into the business—from working with contractors to figuring out financing.

- *Fix It and Flip It.* Written by two authors who have purchased and flipped homes for nearly forty years, this guide offers a wide array of tips on how to follow in their footsteps.
- B4UBuild.com, www.b4ubuild.com. This Web site, designed for those involved in residential construction, offers information about home construction and repair costs, as well as tips for avoiding some of the pitfalls that can accompany home repair. The site has a bookstore with titles of publications on the subject as well.
- Flippinghomes.com, www.flippinghomes.com. Investor and founder Steve Cook offers practical advice and insight on flipping homes.

Inspecting Your Way to Freedom

When Mark Wissing graduated from high school, there was little money for him to continue his education. He managed to eke out a few classes at the local junior college, but not for long. Within a semester or two, he decided to quit. He did manage, however, to land work and receive on-the-job training as an electrician at an area company. It was the starting point for a rich career as a trade worker in which he moved through various occupations—first as a carpenter, then later as an electrician, locksmith, plumber, and a construction project manager.

In one of his last jobs as a journeyman trade worker in the mid-1990s, Wissing worked as a project manager on a seventeen-story high-rise in Chicago. The project was demanding, and Wissing endured twenty-hour days to get the job done. The hours, he decided, were too much. "I decided I had to find something else," he says. That's when Wissing, fifty-three, considered becoming a housing inspector. It certainly made sense. The experience his previous jobs had given him—in trade professions and construction management—conveniently dovetailed with inspecting homes. And Wissing, who lacked a college degree but not strong business acumen, decided to give it a shot.

A few years ago, he earned his inspector's certificate and set up his own house inspection business in Geneva, Illinois, where he lives. The first six months were painfully bleak. "I only did six inspections," Wissing says, recalling how worried he was about succeeding. But then work began to pick up. He targeted real estate offices, making contacts with agents and building a network of referral business. That made all the difference. The next six months, the number of inspections he conducted skyrocketed to fifty-three. This year, Wissing expects his business, which cost about ten thousand dollars to start, will pull in well over six figures in inspection work.

Housing Facts

It's not surprising that once Wissing found a few referrals, his business took off, when you consider the statistics on housing inspection:

- ◆ According to the National Association of Realtors, more than five million homes are sold each year.
- ◆ The US Census notes that 1.5 million new homes are constructed each month.
- ◆ More than seventeen million households move each year, according to the US Postal Service.

Becoming an Inspector

For Wissing, the move to housing inspection seemed obvious—he already knew a lot about the very things he would be inspecting, such as the quality of the carpentry work and electrical systems in a given home. Plus, he had general contracting knowledge that, he says, gives him an advantage over other inspectors.

If you don't have such specialized knowledge, becoming a housing inspector is still an option, but becoming certified in the business is a must. Too many unqualified housing inspectors, Wissing says, are evaluating homes and putting buyers and sellers at risk in the process.

To find out about classes in home inspection, contact your local community college, or check out some of the following resources and guides, which provide information about the business:

- ◆ Housing Inspection Foundation, www.iami.org. This industry group offers information about employment opportunities, as well as the outlook for the profession for the foreseeable future and news about annual conferences for inspectors.
- ◆ National Association of Certified Home Inspectors, www.nachi.org. This industry association's Web site offers information about news and events for housing inspectors as well as online education classes.
- ◆ Inspection Training Associates, www.home-inspect.com. This site offers specific tips and news on inspections for those already in the business as well as training courses in cities nationwide.

- American Society of Home Inspectors, www.ashi.org. A well-organized and easily navigated Web site with myriad information about finding and becoming a home inspector.
- National Property Inspections, Inc., www.npiweb.com. A robust site that offers franchising opportunities for those looking to get into the home inspection business.
- Foundation of Real Estate Appraisers, www.frea.com. This site acts as a liaison among real estate agents, inspectors, lenders, and appraisers, with links to other professionals in the field.
- American Institute of Inspectors, www.inspection.org. A general, nonprofit organization set up to help commercial and residential inspectors, AII offers a Web site that provides conference information for the industry.

Chapter Five

Entrepreneurship Without an MBA

The first time Dana Korey laid eyes on the inside of a classroom, she was ten. Well, there was the brief stint in second grade, but that was for only a week, and only because a truancy officer stopped by Korey's house one day wondering why she wasn't in school. Her parents were dyed-in-the-wool hippies, and Korey's mother continued to embrace the culture well after she was divorced and Dana and her brothers were born. In Miami, where Dana Korey spent her early childhood, any sort of formal education was an afterthought. Topping the list of daily activities were free love and drugs. Her mother's definition of appropriate schooling: "Kids should just enjoy the world and take stuff in. Very the Beatles," Korey says. Whatever that entailed, it didn't involve going to school every day. Instead Korey walked herself to the candy store or otherwise occupied her time with comic books, television, and other time fillers, having been at least taught to read by her mother and stepfather.

The only education she seemed to be getting was that "Frosty," the name of the snowman who appeared in the annual Christmas special once a year, was also the nickname of her mother's bearded, chubby friend who showed up regularly on the family's doorstep with another kind of frosty substance, which was illegal. "We had a yellow submarine and rainbow painted on the front of the house," Korey recalls. "There were a slew of unusual people in and out."

For ten years, Korey's life essentially followed this path, until her father got wind of her absence from school and decided to pull her out of Florida and into school in Arizona, where he lived. There, school officials tested Korey. "One of the fears was, realistically, could I be put into the fifth grade," she says. With tutors hired by her father, Korey was able to catch up rapidly and managed to maintain the school level for her age.

With that precarious start, it is somewhat surprising that Korey made it to college at all. But she did, bouncing from one school to the next for several years, albeit with no real direction and mediocre grades. "I probably got B's in the subjects I enjoyed," she says, not even really remembering. But in those she didn't care for, such as "math and sciences, I got C's, and there might have been a D in there."

Hardly enamored with academia, when an opportunity to go to Europe arose while she was at school, she jumped at the chance. She came back invigorated—but even more disinterested in continuing college. After compiling poor grades and minimal university credit, Korey decided to call it quits. "I managed only three years of credits," she says, before finally giving up.

She accepted an offer to work for a family member's events planning company in Chicago. "I loved the work and the company and what they did, corporate special events," Korey says. "They did all these theme parties. It was cool. I really liked the environment. But I wanted to be able to do more than just be a schlepper and gopher." Essentially, she wanted to become an entrepreneur and work for herself. She got her wish, but not as an events planner. Instead, Korey essentially stumbled into the business she now runs. When friends in San Diego were selling their home and—moments before a stream of potential buyers was due to tour the house—hadn't cleaned up a thing inside, Korey expressed her alarm. "They said, 'We have fifty Realtors coming by.' I said, 'Guys, your house looks like garbage,'" Korey recalls. Selling a home means making it look even more appealing than it actually is. Rock-and-roll posters from ten years ago aren't the way to do that. So Korey helped them rip those down, along with trophies from high school and other items of clutter sitting around the house, stashing much of it in their car trunks. She plunked down a few sets of flowers and candles only moments before the agents arrived.

What happened next shocked Korey even more than the disheveled home had a few moments earlier. Real estate agents, one from Coldwell Banker in particular, began commenting on the house and how spectacular it looked. They wanted to know who'd done the instant makeover. "They thought it was my business," Korey says. "I said, 'You've got to be kidding. It's just one instance.'" But the agents were enthralled, insisting that Korey list herself as an organizational expert in their offices. When she received a few calls after doing so, a thought slowly occurred to her: "Maybe I can do something with this."

On a whim, she planted signs in the ground around upscale neighborhoods offering her services. And people called. To move into the corporate field, she reorganized one cluttered office pro bono for a publisher, who put a small blurb about her services in one of his publications. From that, she received more calls. Over time, she investigated her job more closely and came to realize that not only was this a designated profession, but there was an organization, the National Association of Professional Organizers (NAPO), that could provide her with tips, information, and other services to help her manage her business.

At the same time, *Trading Spaces* and similar home improvement programs were being created at record pace, giving the industry even more exposure. Even unexpected events seemed to drive more business. After 9/11, for example, Korey's requests for business soared. "Everyone was freaking out and in a nesting mode," she says. "They realized while they can't control what was going on outside their home, they want to have a haven and a place of nurturing." That involved reworking and structuring a different environment within their homes. And Korey was happy to help.

Since then her business, which is 65 percent residential and 35 percent commercial, has flourished so much that she's hired teams of people to help her on projects, with annual sales of $750,000. "We have clients that cry and hug us," Korey says in astonishment. "We're really, truly changing their lives."

The irony—that Korey's structureless childhood led to a career of organizing people's lives—is not lost on her. "When I was in my twenties, [my childhood] was something I was pretty ashamed of," she says. "You go on a date and someone says, 'Tell me about grammar school or growing up.' It was not an easy subject. There was a lot of shame." But whatever path that upbringing led her on, it also made her fiercely independent and driven—qualities that undoubtedly helped her become an entrepreneur even without a college degree.

Part of what propelled Korey to become a business owner was the continued feedback she received from so many people who loved what she did. That feedback helped her realize she had a talent for the business. Most people don't have the luxury of having some sort of trial run before becoming an entrepreneur.

But plenty of business owners, particularly those who don't have college degrees, will tell you that opening a business requires, at some point, a leap of faith.

Are You the Next Ray Kroc?

The founder of McDonald's mortgaged his home and cashed in his life savings to launch the world's biggest hamburger chain. His first day of sales netted him $366.12. Today there are more than thirty thousand restaurants worldwide, with annual sales exceeding twenty billion dollars.

But you don't have to build a fast-food chain behemoth to be a satisfied or successful entrepreneur. And you certainly don't have to have a college degree. Ray Kroc didn't. What you do need, however, is a sense of whether you have the inclination to be a business owner, as well as a chance to explore the type of business you'd want to start.

Not unlike a job search, becoming an entrepreneur involves countless hours researching other companies, assessing your strengths and weaknesses, seeking out information from others who have already made the move to open up shop, and considering what kind of money you might expect if you follow in their footsteps.

First things first. Are you even cut out to start a company? Not sure? Think about each of the following questions very carefully, and be completely honest with yourself when answering them. Answering no to even one may mean you're not cut out for this venture:

◆ Am I willing to risk losing the thousands of dollars I'll invest in the business should it flop?

- ◆ Do I have the stamina, enthusiasm, and motivation to work sixteen-hour days, seven days a week if necessary?
- ◆ Am I calm under extreme pressure and able to solve difficult problems on the fly?
- ◆ Am I willing to keep trying should my business flounder initially? More to the point, how long am I willing to stick it out and wait for success? If I'm not profitable within a year, will I keep going or shutter the business?
- ◆ Do I have a strong ability for many of the skills needed to run a business? Do I know how to market and sell? Am I comfortable managing people who are underperformers? Do I know how to create a budget?

What to Sell?

Still want to take the entrepreneurial plunge? Congratulations. Now all you need is to figure out what kind of business you'd like to open. If you're in a job you currently enjoy, but just want to be your own boss, that may be your answer.

When Tony Gierke started Kodiak Corporation, a rubber supply business in Genoa, Illinois, he did so after working for twelve years as a die maker. During that time, he moved up through the ranks to plant manager, but always kept one eye toward possible opportunities to open his own company—one that might be tangential to the industry he'd come to know so well. "I was one of the only persons working in that company that could take a product from inception to departure," says Gierke about the cardboard boxes that were produced from the dies. The company, Triangle Dies and Supplies, a ten-million-dollar-a-year business started by his father-in-law, was "the single largest die shop on the planet," according to Gierke. And a fantastic training ground to open up a complementary business of his own some day.

Gierke was hesitant to make that initial entrepreneurial move until a flyer came floating over the company's fax one day announcing a local company's plans to sell off the rubber cutting portion of its business—along with its equipment, inventory, and list of clients. Fortunately, Gierke's wife, who also worked at Triangle Dies, was the one who first saw that fax, and, after giving first right of refusal to her father, passed the information on to Tony. He was making fifty-two-thousand dollars a year. For just twenty-two thousand ("the asking price was so low it was ridiculous," Gierke says), he bought the company. At the time, it pulled in only $220,000 a year in sales. That was a decade ago. Now sales are over a million dollars a year. "I considered many different things," says Gierke, forty-one, in reference to the type of business he considered starting. "Franchises really didn't interest me. I would much rather have control of my own destiny. With this particular company, it was low-cost to start up, and I knew about the business" already, from years as a die maker, since manufacturing processes between the two businesses are to some degree related. "I felt confident that I could produce the product. It was a really nice fit."

Making the Entrepreneurial Leap

Tony Gierke knew plenty about the business he started already. More importantly, he knew he wanted his own company to remain within that market sector. That's obviously smart. But most people don't enter into a business—as an employee or an owner—with that much knowledge. And even Gierke had his stumbling blocks. He certainly knew manufacturing, but little about the actual red tape he would have to wade through to start the business. "It's pretty complicated," he says. Luckily, there are organizations, magazines, and online resources to guide new entrepreneurs through that first-time confusion.

How to find such information? You can start with the Small Business Administration, www.sba.gov. It houses an enormous volume of information about starting, financing, and managing a company. For help locally, ask your chamber of commerce or other local organizations about groups that may be able to provide assistance. In New York, for example, Project Enterprise, www.projectenterprise.org, is a nonprofit organization that provides microloans and business development services to low-income entrepreneurs in the city.

For sound specific tips and free business advice, check out the following publications and Web sites:

◆ Service Corps of Retired Executives (SCORE), www .score.org. SCORE comprises former business executives who offer free advice to budding entrepreneurs. The Web site offers a searchable database of SCORE offices nationwide as well as links to useful articles and business tips online.

◆ *Inc.* magazine, www.inc.com. With its high concentration of how-to articles covering every imaginable aspect of running a business, this Web site is a must for any new business owner trying to learn the ropes of entrepreneurship.

◆ Bplans.com, www.bplans.com. An invaluable site, bplans .com has step-by-step instructions on how to put together a business plan, as well as tips on other facets of doing business, such as marketing, management, and legal coverage.

Capturing Your Business Vision

Sharon Graham had always wanted to be a police officer— specifically, a California Highway Patrol officer. Her father had worked as one in Los Angeles for twenty-five years. And Graham figured, since she had been a superb athlete in high school (she made it to the state track meet her freshman year), she not only possessed the mental inspiration to do the job, but had the athletic ability and physical stamina to back it up as well. There was just one problem: "My reading comprehension wasn't good," Graham says. During a brief stint at Santa Ana College, a two-year community college in Santa Ana, California, where her father later taught, she would read an entire passage from a classroom text and forget moments later what was in it. Graham found herself dedicating classroom time to daydreaming rather than listening to instruction. A physically hyper woman today whose workout routine often means four-mile runs, Graham found the classroom setting intolerable.

It didn't take long for her to quit out of frustration. She fell back on working, landing in a dry-cleaning shop—an industry she'd fallen into and become intimately familiar with since holding jobs at various cleaners since the age of fifteen. "My dad pushed me to go get a job when I was in high school," says Graham, who received her high school diploma in 1980. "I decided to go to a local shopping center, and it was at Campus Cleaners in Irvine, California," that she got her first job. It would prove to be one of the best decisions Graham ever made—and a launching pad for an extremely lucrative blue-collar career.

The pay was paltry at $3.50 an hour working the counter, but Graham became interested in the business. More to the point, she loved working in business—rather than absorbing lessons in a classroom. "I love to talk to people and interact with people," she says. Behind the dry cleaner's counter, she was getting that stimulation in spades. Slowly she began learning the skills of the business. "I started to learn how to press," she says, picking up other talents as she hopped among jobs at various cleaners. After a while, the names all ran together—Van's Cleaners, Campus Cleaners, Celebrity Cleaners, Bayside Cleaners. Over time she learned how to treat delicate materials, how to press silks. At Sunny Fresh Cleaners, she learned how to treat for spots and stains on various garments. She learned that some cleaners mislead clients, saying they'd tried their best to remove a stain when they'd only spritzed the spot itself, spraying the rest of the garment with deodorant rather than cleaning it. She watched cleaners charging cleaning fees for vinyl products knowing full well they can't be dry cleaned in the first place.

Worse than any lack of ethics, however, were the owners' treatment of employees. At one dry-cleaning shop, the owner was so disrespectful of Graham and other female employees that she had to confront him about his management style. "I must have pulled him outside three times and said, 'Stop talking like this. I'm a human being,'" Graham says. By then she'd been asked to return to Celebrity Cleaners to make twenty dollars an hour as a manager, a cleaning company where she'd previously been fired by the woman owner. Around this time, Graham went through a painful divorce, a situation that was of little concern to her employer, who often was unable to grant Graham the time off she needed for court appointments.

By then, she'd had enough. With a small amount of money inherited after her mother's death, and thousands more from the house settlement after her divorce, Graham decided it was time to go out on her own. In 2000, she plunked ninety-five thousand dollars into a failing cleaning business, in Fountain Valley, a middle-class suburb of Los Angeles, where the owner was making less than ten thousand a year in business. Everyone told her it was a bad business move. Even "my broker told me not to buy it," Graham recalls. Dry cleaning is a luxury and a significant discretionary expense, they told her. People in the Fountain Valley area don't have the money to buy the kind of clothes that need to be dry cleaned, much less the motivation to drive to and pay for the care of those clothes at a failing cleaners.

But Graham had a different business model in mind: She would take the cleaners to the people—and not in Fountain Valley. When opening a dry-cleaning business, "a lot of people look for good locations," Graham says. "They go through bidding wars to get good locations with good clientele." But Graham knew dry cleaning in general is considered an annoying chore that consumers would just as soon do without. The key to dry-cleaning success, Graham thought, was to make the process as effortless and convenient as possible for customers. That meant going to them, rather than asking them to come to her.

So Graham developed a business model in which she picks up dry cleaning from people's homes and delivers it back to them when the clothes are clean. Since clients never see her shop, it doesn't matter that it's in a dingy section of town or a cheesy strip mall. "Irvine charges you 6 percent commission of your gross sales. Newport Beach charges you an arm and a leg," Graham says of higher-income, neighboring towns and the increased cost of conducting business there. In Fountain Valley, she pays a cheaper lease, allowing her to put more money into the business itself. Since opening on Super Bowl weekend in 2000, when she went door-to-door in nearby towns drumming up clients, Graham's business has grown to include six vans, twenty employees, and two thousand customers. Sales average $150,000 a month. In addition, she has focused on growing the business in other ways, landing a role as the official dry cleaner for guests at area hotels (thirteen so far) and local restaurants, where she barters cleaning services for meals.

Finding the Funding

Superb reading comprehension or not, Graham is one savvy businesswoman. And she had enough discipline to save money and finance her business herself. If you're starting out small—very small—that may be an option as well, if you're able to sock away ten to one hundred thousand dollars to get started. Of course, banks, the Small Business Administration, and other organizations offer loans, but they tend to prefer doing so to businesses that have a two- to three-year proven track record. If you've never owned a company before, your chances of securing a loan through one of these avenues may be slim to none. Instead, your best bet on finding the money may be through one of the following sources:

◆ **Friends and family.** Always a good bet, friends, family, colleagues, or others you know well may be eager to help you out and reap a little reward for their small investment in the process. And donations of ten thousand dollars or less are considered gifts by the IRS, and are thus not taxed. Just be careful when doing so—entering into business with a relative has ruined many good friendships.

◆ **Angel investors.** Essentially, angel investors are individuals with money to burn—and they want to burn it on budding businesses they think show promise. Check out *Inc.* magazine's Web site (www.inc.com) for a list of angel investors in various cities around the United States.

◆ **Microloans.** Long used as a way to help entrepreneurs in third-world countries start businesses, the movement has been gaining momentum in the United States as well, but with much larger loans for American entrepreneurs. Generally, they're given to business owners who have trouble securing financing through any other means. Loans can be as little as a thousand dollars or as high as twenty-five thousand. Interest rates on these loans, however, tend to be higher than bank loans.

A Fail-Proof Franchise?

One option to consider if you feel shaky starting your own business from scratch is to open a franchise instead. Doing so means you'll get marketing and management support as well as highly researched demographic information for your area, tips on how to set up your shop, and regular support and education from the national office of whatever franchise it is you open.

For some, joining a franchise is too constricting; it's required that you abide by the standards and regulations of the parent franchise.

In addition, be aware that some of the largest and best-known franchises, such as fast-food chains, can be the most difficult to make succeed. Yes, just about everybody loves McDonald's fries, but you'd be surprised how much money, work, and stress go into making a franchise like that work.

If you really think franchising is the direction for you, at least take advantage of the multitude of Web sites out there that have been set up expressly to help people in your position:

- Franchise.com, www.franchise.com. With its very own "franchise maker," this site helps visitors decide not only if franchising is right for them, but which specific franchise may be their best match.
- FranNet, www.frannet.com. One of the best franchising services available, FranNet offers free advice for those looking to open a franchise.
- FranChoice, www.franchoice.com. Much like FranNet, FranChoice also offers free advice, as well as tests to assess your franchising aptitude.
- The International Franchise Association, www.franchise. org. Want to know something, anything, about franchising? IFA will probably have the answer on this extremely resourceful site.

The Unfranchise Franchise

If you're still not sure about opening a franchise versus going it alone, keep in mind that there are some happy mediums out there—but it may take some heavy-duty Googling to find them. One, New York City's Mudtruck, is a coffee shop started in the back of an old utility truck. Tired of the gentrification that they felt Starbucks brought to the market, Mudtruck's owners built the brand on the notion that individuality is an important factor when conducting business. Their quirky orange trucks can be seen parked curbside at various city locations, while funky cafés have sprung up in a few select locations around town. Now that the owners are looking to branch out in other cities, they want to start franchises (or "friendchises," as they call them)—all of them different. They don't want to dictate to another café owner the parameters of his or her interior or management style any more than they want someone to mandate it to them. Opening up a franchise like this gives new business owners a loose outline of how to set up and run the business without restricting them when it comes to how to run the operation.

Opportunity in Odd Places

One final point to consider regarding business ownership: Be open to opportunities you may not have expected. The man profiled below made a 180 in his career path after his college career fizzled along with his marriage.

It's a long road from the ministry to entrepreneurship, but Glenn Smith made the trip. When he entered St. Louis Christian College in the early 1990s, he had every intention of coming out the other side with a four-year degree and a career as a minister. "I grew up in the church with a really strong family of faith," Smith says. Throughout high school and after, he worked frequently with kids as a volunteer. "It seemed like a logical step to take something that meant quite a bit to me in my personal life and add the joy and experiences that I got in working with kids and make a career out of it," says Smith, who grew up in Bellville, Illinois.

Turns out it wasn't such a logical step. Or at least not feasible. A marriage turned sour while Smith was in school, and he felt a divorced minister wasn't highly employable. Whether that's the case is irrelevant now. After four years in an undergraduate program, Smith, by now interested in pursuing a different career, found himself at a college that offered few other majors outside the ministry. When he called several other universities to see if his credits would transfer, he was disappointed. "Some things like English and communications would transfer, but I had almost four full years of education under my belt, and to find out that I would basically start over at a freshman level...," Smith says, his voice trailing off.

By then he'd sunk about twenty thousand dollars into his education, which, as far as he could tell, was for naught. "These life changes were all thrust upon me at once," he says, recalling the pressure of making a major decision on the spot. He opted to leave school and start a career.

Searching for something, anything, to do, Smith was approached by a friend in the financial services arena. Smith sold insurance, mutual funds, and annuities for a few years. Soon after, he partnered with another business associate to start his own executive recruiting firm, starting out small with low-level executive placements then working their way up. "We were working searches that would pay us from three to six thousand dollars, which is not a whole lot considering you're doing it all free until you make a placement," Smith says. But "we worked that level and then tried to walk our way onto larger searches."

Eventually, he did. Today Smith, the owner of Precise Strategies, Inc., in O'Fallon, Illinois, can make anywhere from fifteen to thirty-five thousand dollars per placement, finding jobs for executives in the financial sector. After his previous partner sold the firm several years ago, Smith decided it was time to branch out on his own. With sixty thousand dollars he'd saved, plus small investments from his parents, Smith took the few clients he had and launched the company out of his house. Since then, his salary has remained steadily in the six figures, from a low of $106,000 a year to a high of $270,000, and he's become so busy that he hires additional recruiters on occasion to help with placements.

Chapter Six

Fields to Consider

If, after investigating several potential career paths, you still have no idea where to start working, you might consider some of the professions listed in this chapter. These professions were picked not necessarily because they're the careers of the moment—though they are currently hyped—but because they have shown consistent growth and market strength over the years, and are projected to add jobs to the labor market for the foreseeable future. With some, such as nursing, struggling to attract applicants, you may even be rewarded with unexpected job perks, offered in an effort to attract more individuals to the profession. If you think any of the talents needed for these jobs match yours, check out the resources listed after each section or revisit some of the researching techniques in chapter 3 to more thoroughly explore these careers and possible jobs within them.

THE LOWDOWN ON HOT CAREERS

Job	Why It's Hot	Median Annual Income or Hourly Rate
Sales	• Ability to control your income • Two million new jobs in sales by 2012 • Ability to work from home	$56,000
Cooking	• Job growth plentiful through 2012 • Greater development of job titles each year • Ability to be creative	$13.34 per hour
Computer sciences	• Immense job growth • Emerging technologies mean more opportunity • Job flexibility	$65,000
Nursing	• More new jobs than any other occupation in the coming years • Personally rewarding work	$48,090
Aviation	• Travel the world on an airline's dime • Short training periods • Plentiful time off	$48,000

A Computer Calling

Ethan Smith made his way to a career in computer science like so many other people these days—through a series of computer certifications. Three semesters at Rensselaer Polytechnic Institute was enough to drive him away. Smith always had every intention of finishing his degree in the institute's engineering school, but in hindsight, he says, "It didn't fit me." Instead, he got "swept up into the world of computers."

Today he's one of many computer professionals who have risen through the ranks not with a bachelor's degree in tow, but with other forms of more practical education bolstering them throughout their careers. In fact, statistics from the Department of Labor reveal that 40 percent of those employed in computer, math, and science fields have only an associate's degree, and many just a high school diploma.

Smith wasn't aware of those numbers when he embarked on his computer career, but he had a strong suspicion that a four-year program wasn't getting him there any faster. And speed was his talent, it turns out. "When I left school, there was another path to recognition in the computer industry that was sort of developing in the dot-com era," he says. "This separate path was product certification." So Smith set out to gain certifications on various platforms within Microsoft Windows 98. Over time, he also obtained certifications in networking equipment produced by Cisco and basic hardware certifications for fixing computers. All of these he obtained at CY Tech Computer School, a technical training school in Albany, New York, that would not confer a four-year degree on Smith for all his efforts.

But he didn't need it. What he needed was more hands-on experience than anything else. "With computers everything is hands-on," he says. "Everything is basically about how fast can you adapt. You sit in a class in school and you go and listen to the teacher and read your book. There's generally no hands-on." That's a mistake for computer majors, he believes. With computers, practical experience is the only way to truly learn the necessary skills to thrive in the computer industry. University lectures "don't allow your mind to fully wrap itself around the concept," because you're listening, not doing. And "if the teacher doesn't know how to transition the material from the book into something you can relate to, that knowledge transfer just doesn't happen."

With his handful of certifications, Smith was easily able to land jobs as a computer specialist at various companies, some of which, admittedly, folded after the dot-com bust. But he persevered, returning to certification programs after each layoff (a wise strategy to remain current on his skills while unemployed), and today works as an IT specialist at IBM making seventy-three thousand dollars a year, with the chance for commissions on certain service jobs for IBM clients.

Computer positions, despite all the chatter regarding outsourcing to India and other places, are not only expected to be a high growth American job market in the coming decade (no surprise there), but will offer "starting salaries that are still quite good, much better than other fields," says Stuart Zweben, associate dean for academic affairs and administration in the college of engineering at Ohio State University in Columbus. "Even compared with other engineering fields, they still rate near the top."

In fact, eight of the ten fastest-growing occupations between now and the year 2010 are computer-related, according to the Bureau of Labor Statistics. The fastest growing, in order of greatest growth, include:

- Computer software engineer, applications.
- Computer support specialist.
- Computer software engineer, systems software.
- Network and computer systems administrator.
- Network systems and data communications analyst.
- Desktop publisher.
- Database administrator.

◆ Computer systems analyst.

◆ Computer and information systems manager.

Even better news: Many of today's computer jobs don't require a bachelor's degree. As companies adopt more sophisticated technology, software programs, and computer systems, demand for people who can fill jobs in computer sciences is predicted to rise through the year 2012, according to the *Occupational Outlook Handbook,* making it easier for those without a college degree to enter the field. But a need to fill positions aside, many companies are simply not requiring a college degree, and are instead comfortable hiring individuals with certifications to fill such positions as computer analysts, database administrators, and computer support specialists, among others.

EDUCATION WITHIN THE SCIENCE AND ENGINEERING FIELDS

Industry	Total Workers	Workers Without a Bachelor's Degree	Percentage of Workers Without a Four-Year Degree
Total	4,682,400	1,036,200	22
Computer and math sciences	1,146,300	454,200	40
Life sciences	295,400	29,000	10
Physical sciences	380,900	24,800	7
Social sciences	363,600	35,300	10
Engineering	2,496,100	492,900	20

Source: US Department of Labor, Bureau of Labor Statistics, US Department of Commerce, Economics and Statistics Administration, US Census Bureau, April 2003 current population survey

Hackers Versus Crackers

Ever since the first virus was unleashed on unsuspecting computer users, the word *hacker* has been used to speak derisively of those who try to break into bank accounts, pilfer money off innocent Web users, and otherwise wreak havoc online, causing companies to spend millions a year to stay one step ahead of them.

The reality, however, is that hackers are actually the good guys. *Crackers,* the derogatory term those within the computer industry have given to high-tech criminals, are actually the ones breaking through security systems and trying to steal identities, among other evil things.

Why is this important? Well, for people who want to learn more about working with computers, hackers are a fantastic way to do that. "The person who got all your bank account numbers and who scams you, those are the people the media calls hackers," says Smith. "But that's a huge misnomer. To hack something is really to learn as much about it as possible." Which is exactly what hackers can do for those new to the industry.

Crackers is the term that IT professionals use for criminals who make a living cracking into other people's accounts. Some industry insiders call them CyberRambos. How to find hackers, not crackers? You can start with *The Hacker Quarterly* (www.2600.com), sold on newsstands and available online. This Web site is most useful for its list of hacker meetings worldwide, including Web links to meeting sites, so you'll know when the next hacker gathering will be in your area.

Making a Foray into Computers

As one of the industries offering the greatest job opportunities and professional growth in the next ten years, the computer field is certainly open to newcomers—and you can find your way in via more than one means. Here are a few of the faster ways.

Find a Niche

"My advice for anybody who's looking to not take the school route is [to] find something, one tiny thing you're excited about, that you absolutely love, and grow with that," Smith says. What he means is that the computer industry is so nuanced and driven by specialty niches these days that the key to success—whether you're in college or moving your way through certifications—is to specialize. Knowing that niche—Cisco-specific knowledge, for example—doesn't mean you should limit yourself to one type of company, however. Instead, it's important, industry experts say, to be able to apply the knowledge from that niche horizontally—across many different types of companies. To find jobs in specific areas of expertise, check out technology-focused job boards (such as the list of Where the Jobs Are: IT provided later in this chapter), particularly those on JustTechJobs.com, where job postings are niche-specific.

Get Certified

One of the fastest ways to a computer career these days may be outside a four-year program. While many companies still value a computer science degree, plenty are quick to chuck the collegiate credentials for more specific, practical—rather than theoretical—training. That's easily obtained at schools that offer certifications in various areas of expertise. Looking for a school in your area? Check out the Web site Computer Training Schools at www.computertrainingschools.com to search for educational facilities by city and state. A link on the site even lists schools targeting newcomers to the industry.

Get in the Back Door

A more strategic way of landing a job in IT may not be by waltzing through the HR department of a company, so to speak, but by networking at various industry events, particularly hacker gatherings, where insiders might shed light on hot jobs and vacant positions. There are plenty to choose from, and some don't cost much at all to attend. Below, a listing of some of the industry regulars:

- ◆ Defcon, www.defcon.org. It's the "largest underground hacking event in the world," according to the organization's Web site. That may be a reference largely to the community set up on the site's home page. But the organization does offer a month-to-month calendar of hacker meetings in various cities around the country.
- ◆ LayerOne, www.layerone.info. This computer security conference in Pasadena, California, costs just sixty dollars to attend. LayerOne brings together Internet security experts worldwide to discuss the latest security issues.
- ◆ AllConferences.Com, www.allconferences.com, is a directory listing specific computer conferences by area of expertise.

◆ If nothing else, Google "computer conferences," and the search engine will deliver its own list of IT conferences and meetings, along with links to dozens of sites that offer similar information.

Know the Industry: Trade Magazines

Besides *The Hacker Quarterly*, check out these other publications:

◆ *Blacklisted 411*, www.blacklisted411.net. Dubbed "the official hacker's magazine," *Blacklisted 411* was established in 1983, and offers more of a running commentary about hacking than hard-hitting news reporting about the computer industry.

◆ *Computerworld*, www.computerworld.com, is an overarching publication that covers the computer industry and all its aspects.

◆ *CSO*, www.csoonline.com. *CSO* stands for "chief security officer," and this magazine covers security-related services and issues facing those executives.

◆ *DM Review*, www.dmreview.com, covers far-reaching trends and issues within the IT industry.

◆ *eWEEK*, www.eweek.com, focuses on news and analysis of programs designed to build e-commerce solutions.

◆ *InfoWorld*, www.infoworld.com. A general-interest technology magazine that covers the nuts and bolts of the industry.

◆ *Security Technology & Design*, www.securityinfowatch.com, covers security technology within a host of professional arenas, such as law enforcement, engineering, and the government.

Ask the Experts

Are you enrolled in some sort of training program at a community college or computer training school? Great. Don't just sit there in class absorbing useful information, though: Make a point of networking with teachers, asking them if they know of any internships, job opportunities, or volunteer projects, even just at the school, that you might qualify for in order to get practical, hands-on experience. Learning and doing in a classroom is great, but it's not the same thing as an actual job. When Ethan Smith was completing his initial certifications, he asked teachers, and was given permission, to "experiment" on school networks. "They let me loose and encouraged the burning desire I had to just experiment and learn," Smith says. That made all the difference in his comfort level with his schools, both in the certification program and when he went to interview for full-time work. Making mistakes in the classroom is one of the greatest advantages of such programs.

Plus, you never know what connections you may make with instructors. After he was laid off following the post-9/11 economic downturn, Smith decided to revisit certification programs while he searched for another job. He impressed the class teachers so much, "I went from no job to full time, since I was actually given an offer while doing certification to teach at the school."

Where the Jobs Are: IT

The beauty of computer jobs is that their listings are plentiful online, with dozens of sites dedicated to computer and technology jobs alone, as opposed to general job boards that list masses of jobs from a multitude of professions. Here are just some of the host of computer job boards out there:

- ◆ Computerwork.com, www.computerwork.com. This national job board offers job listings by state, searchable by skill, job title, description, or location of a particular job. In addition, the site offers information about interviewing techniques, résumé-writing skills, and continuing education and certification links.
- ◆ ComputerJobs.com, www.computerjobs.com. Founded in 1995 "by and for information technology professionals," this excellent job board features high-paying positions, plenty of which don't require a college degree. Job descriptions are intricately detailed—a plus when it comes to crafting résumés and cover letters. Jobs can be searched by job skill, title, or location.
- ◆ Jobs for Programmers, www.prgjobs.com. Essentially self-explanatory, this site offers listings of computer programming jobs and allows job seekers to search positions by interesting benefits, such as whether or not they have a casual dress code, four-day workweek, telecommuting options, and relocation services.
- ◆ Dice, www.dice.com. With 85,904 tech jobs posted, there is certainly plenty of opportunity here for technology job seekers. The site includes a list of what cities offer the hottest tech job market. It offers the latest information and contacts for maneuvering within this profession, including one article titled "How to Know if Your IT Specialty is in Trouble," with tips on how to learn new skills and move on to a higher growth niche.

◆ JustTechJobs.com, www.justtechjobs.com. Since the technology field is so nuanced, it only makes sense that job boards would be as well. That's the whole idea behind JustTechJobs.com, where this incredibly simple (and that's a compliment) Web site makes searching for jobs about as easy as it can get. Plug in your area of expertise—Java, say—and the site takes you to a subpage titled JustJavaJobs .com. The idea is that, rather than making job seekers wade through masses of job postings within various specialties, they should be able to visit a job board focused on just their area of skill. The site offers forty-seven niche boards, including, JustSiebelJobs.com, JustSAPJobs. com, JustCOBOLJobs.com, and JustASPJobs.com.

◆ Tech-Jobs.com, www.tech-jobs.com. This site, launched in 2003 and calling itself "the High-Tech Job Finder," offers basic job search capabilities free to both candidates and employers. Its real value is the section that lists freelance work: Job seekers can review a project and bid out their services to the listing company.

One final resource that should not be missed is the Web site for the National Workforce Center for Emerging Technologies (www.nwcet.org). The site, run by Bellevue Community College in Bellevue, Washington, produces detailed reports about the IT industry, including information about specific industries in which emerging technologies will create more job opportunities.

Closing the Sale

Mike Bender remembers his two years of schooling at the University of Georgia: "I was majoring in marketing and minoring in business administration. But I wasn't minoring in a whole lot of anything other than drinking beer and chasing women."

It's not an uncommon path for many undergraduate men at major state universities. But by December in his second year of school, he had a sobering wake-up call when his father died of a heart attack. His father owned a furniture business, which was suddenly left in the lurch. Bender took the next quarter off to help his mother decide the fate of the company. As he was doing so, one of the company's manufacturers offered to buy the business from Bender's family, then offered Bender a job as a product line rep for a year in Atlanta. "I had no money and at the time they were offering me thirty thousand dollars base," Bender says. "I was like, okay. I can always go back to school. I'm going to take it and run with it."

That's probably the understatement of the century. In 1985, Bender accepted the job and launched what he didn't know at the time would be an incredibly lucrative sales career—but not in the furniture market. That's where he would get his selling feet wet. The real money would come in selling medical equipment and supplies.

After three years in the furniture business, Bender's future wife had had enough of their long-distance relationship. Back in Atlanta, he met a former friend who told him about an opportunity at the medical company where he worked. "I've always been straightforward about not having a college degree," Bender says. "I said, 'I don't have a degree, but if you're still willing to talk, great.' I interviewed for the job, got it, and moved back to Atlanta."

For just over two years, Bender sold surgical equipment and watched his income rise steadily from thirty-eight thousand dollars a year to sixty thousand when he left. "It was a very entry-level job," he says, but it offered him a springboard into higher-paying medical positions. "I started meeting these guys in the operating room that were selling equipment and found out that was where the money is at in the medical business."

Eager to make the same, Bender contacted headhunters hoping they could find him similar work. In 1990, he landed a job at a German medical start-up selling surgical lights, tables, and anesthesia machines. For the next seven years, he built his salary from $48,000 to $240,000. He made similar money at another German medical supply company after that, beginning in 1998, moving, as he had in the previous company, to a management position over time. When that company was bought, he left again. In 2001, he joined his current employer, Trumps, first as a seller, and currently as a manager, where he earns anywhere from $300,000 to upward of $415,000 a year.

Bender believes it's entirely possible to make a strong living in sales, particularly in high growth industries. And though he admits that some prejudices against non-college-grads do arise on occasion—"when you don't have a college degree you can't afford to be half ass," he says—he's rarely hit a hiring roadblock because of it. And his salary has certainly not been held back.

Indeed, sales is a profession that people without college degrees can find much success in, both financially and professionally. The key, experts say, is to find something to sell that you feel passionately about, or to feel absolutely passionate about the process of selling in general.

But Bender warns that those who think they have a passion for selling should realize what they're getting into. For starters, Bender clocks some two hundred thousand air miles a year flying around the country to meet with various clients at hospitals and medical centers. "This is a highly energetic job," Bender says. Introverts need not apply. Selling cycles (and the waiting period for the job's monetary reward in the form of commissions) can be long—eighteen months or longer. Many sellers of medical equipment work out of their homes, which means they need extreme self-discipline and self-motivation. "You have to have the energy to get up and get moving." And you have to maintain that energy, often for more than twelve hours at a stretch. Selling the equipment means hanging out in surgical suites all day, explaining the machine's uses and benefits to doctors and their surgical teams. "Surgeries start at 6:30 AM," Bender says. "You have to be at the hospital at 5:30 AM, which means you have to get up at 4:30. If it's a trial facility, you might be there until eight at night. Then you get back to your hotel room, check your e-mail, and do your follow-up. It's a lot of work. I've been in operating rooms on Friday night at midnight, and in them at Saturday at three in the morning. When the need arises you have to drop what you're doing and go."

Still, the payoff is substantial, as evidenced by Bender's salary. On the plus side, Bender gets to observe cutting-edge technology and the latest advances in surgery and medical treatments. Plus, since he works out of his home, he's often there to hang out with his sons, ten and twelve years old. "I can watch my boys at school, have lunch with them, cut out at 4 PM, and go do something" with his family. That's the appeal of sales when you're not on the road, he says: "You have some freedom."

The Outlook for Sales

In 2002, sales accounted for 1.9 million jobs in America. That number is expected to rise quickly by 2012, as older workers retire and those who tire of selling opt out for other professions.

How much a salesperson earns varies widely, depending upon what you sell and where you live. But starting salaries of fifty thousand are common—and that's before commissions kick in.

Ironically, since sales has historically been a profession where college degrees were not required, more and more universities are developing sales majors and designated selling centers where students learn how to craft a pitch, study techniques, and even travel to participate in national selling competitions. The good news for those who want to skip the four-year sales degree, however, is that some of these institutions offer sales education for those who simply want to hone their selling skills. They include:

- ◆ Russ Berrie Institute for Professional Sales, William Patterson University (www.wpunj.edu/rbisales/default .html). The school offers a certificate program, Fundamentals of Professional Selling, that starts with cold calling and takes participants through closing a deal.

- ◆ Fisher Institute for Professional Selling, University of Akron, Ohio. The school offers certificates in professional selling that can be obtained after just fifteen credit hours, without completing a bachelor's degree. Check out www.uakron.edu/colleges/cba/institutes/fisher/index .php for the program details.

- ◆ H. H. Gregg Center for Professional Selling, Ball State University, Muncie, Indiana (www.bsu.edu/salescenter), offers a sales fair open to those willing to pay one hundred dollars to get in. That's a small price to obtain access to recruiters from sixty companies there for the express purpose of hiring the next sales superstars for internships and full-time positions. Impress them with your personality and abilities, and you stand a good chance of landing an offer or two. Can't attend the fair? If nothing else, check out the site's links to job boards listing sales positions.

◆ The Sales Excellence Institute, University of Houston (www.salesexcellence.org), offers a three-semester certificate in professional selling for current professionals or students.

The Nature of the Work

Before taking advantage of one of these programs or plunging headfirst into the sales job market itself, it's important to consider what it takes to sell. Love the idea of commissions so robust they blow the earnings ceiling sky-high? Then you'd better know how to motivate people to buy.

Unlike many other professions, where, to succeed, it's important to absolutely love what you do, a top seller's passion is frequently directed more toward the art of the close itself than toward the actual item sold. Sure, it definitely helps to be fascinated with the product you're pushing. But history has shown that those who really excel in the sales profession are largely driven by the desire to be persuasive, convince prospects to buy, and, ultimately, make lots of money.

To get there, you'll need a few crucial personality ingredients, along with some understanding of what the working conditions are like. Most important? Learn to love rejection. Nine times out of ten, sellers will hear the word *no* when they move to close the deal. But that one *yes* can really pay off. If you're considering a career in sales, make sure you have a thick skin—rejection is a part of the job, but it's not personal. Those who internalize that rejection will wither in the field.

It's also crucial not to drop the ball. Ask any top sellers and they'll tell you that selling is a numbers game—the more calls you make, the closer you get to a sale. Salespeople need to be highly organized, efficient with their time, persistent with follow-up, and—most importantly—not afraid to pick up the phone and make cold calls.

You'll need to understand the deal behind the deal as well. Too many people enter the sales profession with the notion that selling is a matter of rattling off features to prospects in the hope that they'll be wowed by the details. The reality is that today's sales reps are as much business consultants as pitchmen. They need to understand not only the intricacies of their product or service, but also how it can solve the problems of their clients. That means studying industries into which you sell, and knowing, backward and forward, the problems, latest developments, and key areas of growth for every company you approach for business.

Finally, you'll need to get used to working thirty thousand feet up. Selling is about building relationships—and that means meeting face-to-face. Don't like to travel or be away from home? Then abandon the notion of sales immediately. Some sales jobs require far more or less travel than others, depending upon the territory, company, and nature of the business in which you're selling. But almost all require getting in a car or plane for long hauls through territories. One of the perks, of course, is that salespeople rack up frequent traveler points faster than almost any other professionals. Just make sure you don't mind making hotel rooms a regular part of your work schedule.

How to Learn More

A few key sales publications and organizations exist, with articles that cover both the basics and intricacies of more sophisticated selling strategies, as well as the latest developments within the profession:

- *Sales & Marketing Management* magazine, www .salesandmarketing.com. Around for dozens of years, *Sales & Marketing Management* is a robust monthly magazine that offers tips on selling techniques, articles on professional trends, and features about specific companies. In addition, the magazine's Web site includes an extremely useful section called "Personal Career," which covers work–life balance issues, travel news, personal finance, and image advice. Through a partnership with CareerBuilder, the magazine also offers a career center link with more than four hundred thousand job listings from potential employers.
- *Selling Power* magazine, www.sellingpower.com. A longstanding publication, *Selling Power,* like its competitor *Sales & Marketing Management,* is one of the most popularly read publications in the field, providing general information about selling strategies and news.
- Strategic Account Management Association (SAMA), www.strategicaccounts.org. Strategic account managers are sellers working on large, complex sales from one business to another. SAMA addresses the sellers in this sector of sales, offering research, job postings, and links to other informational sources.
- Sales & Marketing Executives International (SMEI), www.smei.org. The profession's main association, SMEI offers research, information about professional events, and job listings nationwide, largely for business-to-business sales.

- Direct Selling Association (DSA), www.dsa.org. The Direct Selling Association focuses on consumer sales, offering research, and professional news to those who work for companies that sell to consumers directly.
- Sales Vault, www.salesvault.com. This site is an information-packed guide to the entire sales profession with articles, links to books, career advice, seminars, and, of course, job listings.

Where the Jobs Are: Sales

Unlike a lot of professions where internships are a great way to snag a full-time job, sales departments aren't as keen to bring interns under their wing and nurture them into great sellers. They want top performers yesterday, and they're more interested in training those they think will stick around for a significant length of time. That said, the good news about the sales job market is that there are a surplus of entry-level positions just waiting to be filled for selling newbies, eager to hit the phones in a cold-calling fury. In addition, as with most professions, there are job boards specifically designed for those interested in a career in sales.

- SalesJobs, www.salesjobs.com. No surprise that a site with a name this obvious would develop, given the opportunities that exist now and will only increase. Job listings are searchable on this highly organized site by industry, location, or company. The site's best asset, however, may be the actual résumés it posts, giving detailed examples of how to structure a sales résumé and what type of information to include. In addition, SalesJobs includes fun advice such as what to wear and interviewing tips.

◆ MarketingJobs.com, www.marketingjobs.com. Since sales and marketing often go hand in hand, you'll find many sales postings listed on sites that also focus on the marketing profession. This one is no different, listing jobs nationwide as well as helpful career advice.

◆ Medzilla, www.medzilla.com. Combine the growing fields of medicine, biotechnology, and sales, and you'll get a rich Web site full of job postings. Such is the idea behind Medzilla, which highlights sales positions at pharmaceutical companies, biotech firms, and health care organizations. The site's setup is interesting. While jobs can be searched by keyword, they can also be perused by company. Just click on a corporate logo and view all the postings for that particular business—a great job search method for those interested in medical sales specifically, and a given company in particular.

◆ SalesTrax, www.salestrax.com. This site is dedicated to helping people find pharmaceutical, financial, technology, business, and industrial sales jobs. It lists career fairs in cities around the country and their corresponding dates. The site also includes career advice and a job database searchable by keywords.

◆ iHireSalesPeople, www.ihiresalespeople.com. A highly organized, comprehensive job board, iHireSalesPeople offers thousands of job postings for candidates and résumés for companies to review.

Fire Up the Grill

Ken Addington is an executive chef at a trendy New York restaurant. Not that you would have predicted that career path from his childhood, which was spent largely out of the kitchen. "I baked a little bit with my mom, and [I'm] still not much of a home cook, to be honest," he says. Even so, he had a natural inclination to cook, which he discovered at sixteen. That's when Addington entered a city internship program through his high school, moving through several organizations, including groups such as the National Organization for Women, photography labs, and record companies, until cooking caught his interest. "It was a good environment and it was fun," recalls Addington, now the executive chef for Bette, a chic restaurant on the West Side of Manhattan. "It was exciting with a lot of fire and knives and yelling. The rush of it all" was appealing to Addington. And when he later discovered the creativity that could come with the job, he was hooked.

Rather than pay his dues in cooking schools, of which New York has plenty, Addington picked up his skills by moving through kitchens, learning as he went. In fact, finding a spot under the tutelage of a "good chef" in a Brooklyn restaurant when he first entered the profession was the key to a steep learning curve, he says. Doing so also gave him a better sense of the profession than if he'd gone straight to cooking school. "It's important to step into it first," says Addington, who now makes close to six figures a year.

For people without a college degree, cooking offers a world of opportunity. Employing more than 12.2 million people, the restaurant industry is the largest private-sector employer in the United States, according to the National Restaurant Association, with 65 percent of those working in the business having a high school degree or less. And 1.8 million new jobs are expected to be added to the profession by the year 2014.

But for those considering cooking careers—and the jobs can be plentiful with decent pay for those who do—there are a few things to consider. For starters, the best way to learn how to be a chef is often on the job, say many who are in the industry. In cooking schools, education is sometimes as much about theory as it is time in the kitchen. Addington says he's hired students straight out of cooking schools who "don't even know how to sharpen knives."

That said, there are plenty of good educational cooking centers. Just make sure you find one that offers realistic practical training. School prices can range wildly—from several thousand dollars to more than forty thousand dollars for a two-year degree in cooking from a culinary institute. That's a lot of money to toss around when the same skills could be learned for free (or, rather, for pay) somewhere on the job. If you're timid about jumping feetfirst into a restaurant, a cooking school may be the most appropriate and comfortable choice. If nothing else, schools, which do teach a substantial amount of practical skills depending upon where you go, also give students a good sense of the restaurant industry before they enter the job market. (But first, be sure to check out the tips below on how to pick a cooking school.)

In addition, those within the industry warn that cooking in a restaurant—from a tiny, five-star affair to a megachain Red Lobster—is rarely easy, and almost never glamorous. It's not the breezy or high-powered environment portrayed on cooking shows or reality TV programs. In fact, it's usually hard labor, over a hot and greasy stove, with immense pressure and deadlines to get food out to tables on time. Fall behind in your duties and you'll undoubtedly get blasted by the head chef or manager.

Industry turnover is high. Stick around the same kitchen for more than a couple of years and you'll be considered an old-timer. At the same time, jobs are plentiful—at least right now. When Addington left New York for Australia several years ago, he came back after 9/11 expecting to find a sleepy restaurant industry stateside. That wasn't the case. "There is so much work" to be had in places like New York that "it's actually a struggle to get good help." That means opportunities abound for those who do decide to give the field a shot.

If that's you, you'll need to leave your ego at the door. As the saying goes, if you can't handle the heat, get out of the kitchen. Cooking can "feel like a very inhumane business," Addington says. "There's a lot of yelling and speaking to people rudely." Maybe because the industry has tolerated such attitudes in high-intensity kitchens nationwide, it's become an accepted part of the business where that's not the case in other professions. "Humility is really important," Addington notes. Those who are sensitive or have thin skin should probably choose another line of work.

Another consideration for would-be chefs: Organization is crucial. "This is not the kind of job where if you don't have time to get the soup on you can do it tomorrow, because people want to eat the soup tonight," Addington says. Point well taken. But when you're a chef, being fast, efficient, and organized doesn't stop in the kitchen. Paperwork has to be organized and taken care of nightly to make sure restaurant supplies and operations are running smoothly. In that sense, operations can change on a dime, depending on staff or supply issues. Being flexible is a job requirement.

Finally, learn to accept the ground floor. In this industry, everyone pays their dues; there are very few shortcuts to the title of executive chef. Those who made it to the top all started as line chefs, slaving away and catching heat for doing so. You'll need to do the same, for rock-bottom wages. But for those who climb their way to the top after a decade or more in the business, the pay for an executive chef can easily reach $80,000, and as much as $250,000 for top chefs in major cities.

How to Pick a Cooking School

If you feel cooking school is your best bet, go for it. But remember, cooking programs are offered at a variety of educational centers, from private cooking classes to major universities; you can even earn a doctorate in the subject. Be sure you're picking the best school for your needs. To assess the sophistication and quality of training at the school you're considering, you might want to ask yourself—or better yet, the school—some of the following questions:

- Are the school's kitchens modern, large, and similar to those I'll be working in at a restaurant?
- How much time is spent on theory versus hands-on experience in each class?
- Does the student-to-teacher ratio allow for a fair amount of personal instruction during each class?
- Is your school accredited?
- Do you have a strong record of placing students in jobs upon completion of their courses?
- Does your school offer financial assistance?
- Does your school offer classes in other aspects of chef duties, such as business operations?

◆ Can I get the contact information of half a dozen former
students and ask them what they thought of your program? How helpful was it to getting a job in the industry? Did the instruction adequately prepare them for
their current job?

The Kitchen as Classroom

If you prefer to skip formal culinary school—and its sometimes
steep tuition—you can head straight to your nearest restaurant instead. When he started out, Addington did so through
internship programs. They may not all pay, but they're a great
way to get inside a working kitchen and get a sense of the skills
needed to work there as well as the pace of work a job as a chef
demands.

If you feel cooking school is the best route for your experience
and comfort level, you might want to skip the larger programs.
Landing a spot at the Culinary Institute of America may sound
impressive, but you might actually learn more at a smaller cooking school, such as one only offered in your city by local chefs.
Doing so can mean more intimate classes, greater practical experience, and a better rapport with an instructor, who might be
more likely to pass on job referrals.

The Alternative Chef

Want to become a chef but stay out of a traditional chain or
fine-dining kitchen? There are plenty of options. Thousands of
hotels, for example, need chefs to run their food and beverage
services, as do corporate kitchens such as Bear Stearns, which
offers elegant dining to a select group of executives on the top

of its Park Avenue office building. But there are also a growing number of nontraditional chef positions that may not require paying your dues in the back of Bennigan's while the head chef is breathing down your neck to speed up your delivery.

For families who can afford it, hiring a private chef is a fantastic luxury. And for chefs who enter this line of work, the experience can be liberating, since you'll often be charged with creating menus for your clients, and the pay can be astounding—more than six figures at the high end—depending on how wealthy your client family is. One thing to consider: Private chefs have one client—the family they cook for. So working intimately with one group is something you should definitely enjoy.

If being a private chef feels a little too intensive for you, becoming a personal chef may be more appealing. Here, chefs are essentially their own bosses, marketing their culinary talents to a handful of clients who hire them to cook individual meals. Celebrities are big on this, and personal chefs can net fifty thousand dollars or more a year.

A final thought: entertainment chef. From in-home cooking classes (at clients' homes) to TV appearances, entertainment cooking is one of the fastest-growing fields for those in the culinary arts. Companies such as Culinary Inspirations offer classes specifically designed to educate students on how to become entertainment chefs.

Where the Jobs Are: Cooking

Looking for a top culinary school or more education about the business? Industry standouts include the Culinary Institute of America, Johnson & Wales University, New England Culinary Institute, the French Culinary Institute, and the Restaurant School at Walnut Hill College, among others. But that doesn't mean you can't find great training elsewhere. And with cooking catching fire (sorry for the pun) as a profession today, there are plenty of Web sites to help would-be chefs sort through all the educational options. A few stellar sites include the following:

- ◆ All Culinary Schools, www.allculinaryschools.com. This comprehensive, easy-to-navigate Web site includes summaries of dozens of schools. In addition, it offers helpful tips about the industry in general.
- ◆ Peterson's Culinary Schools, www.petersons.com/culinary. Sponsored by educational resource company Thomson Learning, this site offers a list of nearly a hundred highly respected cooking schools in the United States and abroad. The real value of this site is the research put into its Web content. Click on a school description and you can read about the physical characteristics of the school's kitchen, get a demographic profile of the average student, read a rundown of instructors' credentials, and get a listing of fees, including average area housing costs.
- ◆ CookingSchools101.com, www.cookingschools101.com. This Web site is essentially a compilation of other sites out there for those with a culinary interest. But it also provides a seemingly endless array of articles, facts, and links to every aspect of the food and beverage industry—from sommelier jobs to chef uniforms.
- ◆ Culinary Business Academy, www.culinarybusiness.com. This inviting, easily navigated site is fantastic for background information on different sectors of the culinary

industry, offering tips and instruction on how to become a personal chef, for example, or how to become a caterer.

◆ Hireachef.com, www.hireachef.com. Managed by Kreotek, LLC, a company that creates Web and software programs for personal and other types of chefs, hireachef is largely a job board for personal chefs looking for work as well as individuals trying to hire them.

◆ US Personal Chef Association (USPCA), www.uspca.com. Probably the most logical place to get started as a personal chef, the USPCA Web site provides tips on entering the field as well as information that could set a chef apart—such as becoming professionally certified. Memberships to USPCA, ranging from seventy-nine to six hundred dollars a year, bring various benefits, such as liability insurance, professional software, and educational conferences.

◆ International Association of Culinary Professionals, www.iacp.com. Another industry association, but with more of an emphasis on culinary jobs in general. The site offers information about educational conferences as well as job postings nationwide.

◆ National Restaurant Association (NRA), www.restaurant. org. Considered the go-to site for all jobs and topics dealing with restaurants, the NRA's Web site also includes a restaurant job bank, industry research, and career advice.

Florence Nightingale Was On to Something

Nursing has long been a highly touted profession for job seekers—not because many people were rushing to join the field, but because they weren't. The shortage of applicants to fill nursing

jobs has been such a problem in recent years that signing bonuses
upward of several thousand dollars, and perks for nurses as well
as their families, are common these days. In addition, some health
care facilities are offering to cover some educational expenses to
entice people into the profession.

All of this means the field is wide open for those who want to
enter. With 2.3 million jobs, nurses make up the largest sector of
the American health care market. That's only going to increase,
as the field is projected to have greater job growth than any
other profession in the next decade. For those who skipped college, the good news is this: Plenty of nursing jobs don't require
a four-year degree.

Nursing's Many Faces

Nurses are needed everywhere—from the emergency room to
the workplace. Some of the most common environments for
nursing include:

- ◆ **Hospitals.** Hospitals employ the largest number of nurses
  nationwide. Nurses here generally specialize, say, in car-
  diac care, the emergency room, or intensive care. Strong
  job growth is expected to occur particularly in hospital
  outpatient centers that offer same-day surgery and other
  services that don't require overnight stays.
- ◆ **Doctors' offices.** Physician's offices and other outpatient
  medical centers employ nearly forty-five thousand nurses
  nationwide. Hours here are generally better than in hospitals, since doctors' offices close at the end of the day.
- ◆ **Homes.** Working in homes can offer pleasant job surroundings and a personal relationship with clients that

nurses in other work locations don't enjoy. In addition, home health nurses have a lot of autonomy and independence, and must generalize in nursing care, rather than become specialists, as they might in a hospital.

◆ **Schools and companies.** Nurses working in educational, corporate, or government environments not only assist patients with health concerns but also often organize educational health fairs and produce educational materials to keep the public aware of various health issues and news.

◆ **Work sites.** Nurses at work sites offer not only acute care services but also health counseling and preventive care, such as inoculations.

Bedpans or Botox?

Depending on where you work and with what patients, the responsibilities of nursing can vary widely—from easing bedpans out from under patients in post-op recovery to helping celebrities out the door after minor surgery at a Beverly Hills doctor's office. Regardless of the environment in which you work, however, all nursing jobs deliver some similar experiences and require some particular personality characteristics.

First and foremost, it's important to consider that nursing is not a desk job. Nurses spend long days on their feet, standing over patients or walking through hospitals to help deliver patient care. The activity is certainly less than the demands of, say, heavy construction, but being a nurse rarely means sitting behind a counter triaging patients all day.

You must also be prepared to keep your pager close. Especially if you work in a hospital, you never know when accidents or tragedies may occur, requiring additional staff. When traumas do occur, you may be on call to race to operating rooms at all hours of the day.

Hazards lurk. Besides diseases that are obviously appearing in medical centers everywhere, nursing exposes professionals to electrical shocks, radiation, and other hazards found in medical facilities.

Finally, remember that in this industry, compassion is key. Since they're working with patients who may be seriously ill or mentally unstable, nurses often need patience and sensitivity to people's various conditions. Helping them through those issues is one of the most rewarding experiences for those who enter this occupation.

A Course of Study

In every state, nurses must complete a nursing program and pass a licensing exam. Luckily, there are nursing programs at community colleges and hospitals that take less time and cost significantly less money than a four-year degree. In fact, while plenty of nurses are getting bachelor's degrees, a large portion of them are becoming educated through community colleges as well.

THE EDUCATIONAL PATH TO NURSING

Highest Degree Received	Percentage of Registered Nurses with Degrees
Baccalaureate degree	34
Associate's degree	34
Diploma program	18
Master's degree	13

Source: National Sample Survey of Registered Nurses, 2004

At community colleges, nursing students receive an associate's degree in nursing (ADN) after two or three years of study. Though the number of hospitals that offer nursing programs has decreased dramatically in the last twenty years (from more than eight hundred in the 1970s to fewer than one hundred today), it's still an option for the moment. Hospitals offer diploma programs in nursing that generally last three years. These days, even online programs are available. Check out All Nursing Schools, www.allnursingschools.com/faqs/programs.php. This site lists hundred of educational centers as well as information about more unusual types of nursing occupations.

Other Helpful Sites

The nursing profession offers a host of Web sites dedicated to the news and issues of nursing as well as helping nurses further their education and career opportunities:

◆ Health Resources and Services Administration, www .hrsa.gov. More of a research tool than a career resource, the government's site is still packed with valuable information about potential earnings and employment settings for those considering a career in nursing.

◆ American Nurses Association, www.nursingworld.org. The site contains news and events about nursing as well as a link to the American Nurses Credentialing Center, where visitors can learn about various nursing certifications.

◆ American Academy of Nursing, www.aannet.org. An umbrella industry organization created to keep those in the profession abreast of the latest trends and issues within the field of nursing.

Where the Jobs Are: Nursing

With so many openings and so few nurses, it's no wonder there
are plenty of job boards online with dozens of opportunities for
those looking to land a job. Here's a sampling:

◆ NurseJobs.com, www.nursejobs.com. This site features
more than twelve thousand nursing jobs searchable
by state, work environment, medical specialty, type of
employment (full time or part time), and even work eli-
gibility status.

◆ Nursing Jobs, www.nursingjobs.org. This site offers job
searches by state as well as a blog for nurses looking to
reach out to others with comments or questions about
the profession.

◆ Nurse-Recruiter.com, www.nurse-recruiter.com. Created
"for nurses by nurses," this site breaks nursing jobs down
into environmental and hierarchical categories, where
job seekers can look for assignments from summer camp
work to travel nursing jobs.

◆ Nursing-Jobs.us, www.nursing-jobs.us. Free registration
offers users of this site access to thousands of nursing
jobs nationwide as well as an online nursing forum.

◆ Access Nurses, www.accessnurses.com. Like most nursing Web sites, this job board offers thousands of job
opportunities. But it also, in a highly organized and easy-
to-navigate manner, offers listings for additional nursing
work under the category of per diem nursing jobs, where
nurses can make up to five hundred dollars on their days
off—a not uncommon practice. The Department of

Labor reports that about one in ten nurses have more
than one job.

◆ Nurses123, www.nurses123.com. This friendly site
offers listings for jobs, but also information about
news about nursing, an online forum for those in the
profession to discuss issues, and a list of nursing job
fairs.

Piloting a New Career

With airlines beleaguered by striking workers, bankruptcies,
skyrocketing fuel costs, and the constant threat of terrorism, it
would seem to be the industry to avoid like the plague. But the
Department of Labor predicts that job growth for people within
aviation will increase as significantly as any other occupation
in the next several years. And for those interested in a career
in and around planes, you can't beat the perks—like seeing the
world on the airline's dime.

For those with a passion for flying, it's surprisingly easy to
become qualified as a commercial pilot on regional jets, working for a major carrier. Flight training at the Regional Airline
Academy, in Deland, Florida, for example, is only a fourteen-
month program, taking people who are novices and turning
them into commercial pilots. One drawback: That ability to fly
won't come cheap. The program costs between sixty and
seventy-three thousand dollars, depending on which classes you
choose to take, says Shane Williams, marketing director for the
organization. But on the upside, "We place 98 percent of our
pilots that graduate from the program with an actual regional

carrier." Other academies have similar partnerships and placement records. At Regional Airline Academy, new graduates
might land jobs with American Eagle, the regional airline for
American Airlines, or Express Jet, the carrier for Continental
Airlines, both of which maintain recruiting partnerships with
the academy, as do other airlines.

Landing the Job

Besides logging between five hundred and seven hundred hours
of flying time, qualifying to work as a commercial pilot usually requires a high school diploma or GED, a significant background check to pass more rigid airport security standards
today, a physical, and a clean criminal record with no arrests for
things like DUI. All pilots must pass a written exam before they
can fly commercially, and some airlines may have additional
exams of their own to test the abilities of job candidates.

Many students are recent high school graduates, but students
as old as forty have entered Regional Airline Academy with no
prior flying experience and come out with full-time jobs. Pay for
regional pilots starts low—as low as twenty-two thousand dollars the first year—but rises quickly with each year of employment. Third-year pilots can earn as much as forty thousand a
year, while those with eight years of flying under their belts can
expect to take home upward of eighty. And pilots with more
seniority often get to choose their schedules and flights, in addition to enjoying as much as half of each month off from work.
Of course, since commercial pilots are required to retire at age
sixty, the older you are as a student, the more you shorten your
career and limit your earning potential.

The Right Academy

With hundreds of pilot training academies nationwide, choosing the right one can be difficult—and a career killer if you select one that has poor or nonexistent recruiting relationships with airlines. Experts suggest looking into schools in the Southeast and Southwest, since weather conditions there allow for more flying days on average each year. "In Florida, we have about 340 good flying days a year," says the Regional Airline Academy's Williams.

If you know nothing about aviation, flight schools, or the airline industry, you could get duped and spend a lot of money becoming a pilot with no job prospects upon graduation. How to pick the right flight school? Start by asking the school you're considering the following questions:

- ◆ Do you specifically prepare your students for commercial airline careers?
- ◆ How many hours of flying time will I get in your program? At least eight flights a week, or one a day minimum, is ideal, but more is better.
- ◆ Do you have recruiting partnerships with major carriers?
- ◆ What's your job placement rate for graduates?
- ◆ What flying experience do your instructors have?
- ◆ Do you have flight simulators for jets such as 737s or CRJ simulators?
- ◆ Is your school approved by the Federal Aviation Administration (FAA)?

For a list of FAA-approved schools, and more information about becoming a pilot, as well as a database in

which to search for schools by city and state, go to www.faa
.gov/education_research/training/pilot_schools.

Aviation's Additional Callings

Not into piloting the plane? It used to be that staffing an air
traffic control tower was an ideal, albeit highly stressful,
career choice for an aviation enthusiast who didn't have a college degree. But most airports now require a four-year degree
to become a controller. Still, there are plenty of other ways to
become involved in the airline industry. Two with high earnings
and job opportunity potential are detailed next.

Flight Attendant

Some may write off flight attendants as glorified waiters in the sky,
but most normal restaurant servers don't get to stroll around Paris
when their shift is over. And though entry-level salaries can be
quite low—twenty thousand dollars or less—the earnings potential with years of seniority can top out at ninety-one thousand or
more. In addition, like pilots, flight attendants enjoy days off at a
stretch during each month, though they can often be called to work
at a moment's notice—even in the middle of the night—should a
co-worker call in sick or be unable to make a flight.

Airlines conduct their own training of flight attendants, and
though some prefer a college degree, there are still plenty of
opportunities for jobs as a flight attendant for those with an
associate's degree, a high school diploma, or a GED. To apply
for a flight attendant training program with an airline, check
out these pages on the country's major airline Web sites:

- American: www.aacareers.com.
- Delta: www.delta.com/about_delta/delta_employment_opportunities/index.jsp.
- Continental: www.continental.com/company/career/flightattendant.asp.
- United: www.united.com/page/article/0,6722,51394,00.html.
- Northwest: www.nwa.com/corpinfo/career/summary.html.
- JetBlue: http://jetblue.recruitmax.com/ENG/candidates.
- Southwest: www.southwest.com/careers/careers.html.
- US Airways: www2.usairways.com/awa/content/aboutus/employment/default.aspx.

Airline Mechanic

If you love airplanes and aviation, working as a mechanic can be an inspiring and rewarding position—your expertise is helping passengers get to where they need to go. The pressure of working against the clock to maintain flight schedules and keep passengers happy can be exhilarating. But doing so can also mean working long hours, kneeling or hunched over in awkward positions atop scaffolding or outdoors in inclement weather. Still, job growth in this industry is expected to remain strong as older workers exit their jobs. And pay can climb as high as thirty dollars an hour.

Individuals with a high school diploma or GED can enter one of the FAA's 170 aviation maintenance technician schools and become certified to work in the industry within one to two years. Written and oral exams administered by the FAA are required

for employment. Check out the FAA's Web site, www.faa.gov/
mechanics/training, for information on becoming an airline
mechanic as well as how to find training schools.

Where the Jobs Are: Aviation

For general information about where to find careers in aviation, the following Web sites offer job listings, articles about
the aviation industry, and information on training for various
positions:

♦ AirlineCareer.com, www.airlinecareer.com.
♦ Thirty Thousand Feet, www.thirtythousandfeet.com.
♦ Airline Inflight, www.airlineinflight.com.

Chapter Seven

The Blue-Collar Boom

Somewhere within his ninth-grade year, Art Lewis realized he wanted to be a cop. "I did a ride-along on a job training day in Flint, Michigan," while in high school, Lewis remembers. "Flint has an extremely high crime rate." Indeed it does. In 2004, Flint held the second highest violent crime rate of any US city. The night Lewis rode in the back of a police cruiser with Flint police in the early 1980s, the city's crime record did not disappoint. "It was the day before Halloween, which they call devil's night," Lewis says. "The city had over three hundred fires that night set by vandals, and two murders—one still unsolved to this day."

Lewis loved it that the police officers didn't confine him to the car at crime scenes. "Once they knew the scene was safe, they allowed me to tag along to see what's going on." Back at the station, "they involved me in paperwork and the booking process, and walked me through" how it works.

He was hooked. Only problem: In Michigan, budding police officers have to be sponsored by a police agency or have a bachelor's degree to get into the academy. Instead, Lewis became a paramedic, working for one of Flint's private ambulance companies before injuring himself on the job and being forced to leave. Plus, working as a paramedic only paid nine dollars an hour in Michigan. "On the road, I was an extension of the physician" back in the emergency room, "but I only got paid one one-hundredth of his salary," Lewis says.

In 1999, he left Michigan and moved to Florida, where he needed only a high school diploma to enroll in one of the state's training academies. After rethinking his profession for several years, Lewis graduated from a five-month program at the Criminal Justice Institute at Seminole Community College in Sanford, Florida, and accepted an offer from the Longwood Police Department, a city nearby. His income will start at thirty-eight thousand dollars a year, but will be well beyond fifty thousand within ten years, he says.

The (Blue) Light at the End of the Tunnel

Think blue-collar jobs involve backbreaking work for slave wages? Consider this joke: An electrician walks into an attorney's home and spends five minutes rejiggering his faulty wiring. When he's done, he hands the lawyer a bill.

"Five hundred dollars?" the attorney yells, shocked. "That's outrageous. I'm a lawyer, and even I don't make that much."

The electrician turns to the lawyer and says, "Neither did I when I was an attorney."

It's a humorous tale told often these days, and its point is well taken: The blue-collar job market is robust, full of opportunity, and highly lucrative for those who love manual labor. In construction alone, for example, an estimated shortage of

250,000 jobs plagues the industry right now, a number that will creep over 1 million by the year 2012.

As you'll discover in this chapter, trade jobs are, as always, still a career sector dominated by men. But that's been changing in the past few decades, and more so every year. These days, women are gaining ground on their male counterparts, landing positions in construction, maritime work, law enforcement, transportation, and countless other fields. In construction, for example, "with the labor shortage we're facing, there are plenty of openings and it's a great career choice for women," says Cassandra Lopez, marketing director for the National Association of Women in Construction.

Though certain trade jobs in manufacturing, particularly in areas such as clothing production, have moved offshore, some work—construction, for instance—must be done domestically, for obvious reasons.

Part of the reason so many blue-collar jobs can expect high growth in the next several years is that many people don't consider them as their first career choice. But even high-profile blue-collar jobs with a more glamorous aura, such as police work and firefighting, are expected to offer continued growth for jobs through 2012, particularly in smaller cities and rural areas, as boomers retire and high turnover contributes to positions needing to be filled.

"Law enforcement is very, very desperate for good people," says Richard Weinblatt, the police academy manager at Seminole Community College, where Art Lewis went through his training, adding that some of the most exciting law enforcement work is found in small towns in the Southwest or Southeast, where smaller departments ask cops to do more. Departments like the NYPD in New York rarely offer the action-packed positions portrayed on shows like *Cops,* according to Weinblatt, because with a force of nearly forty thousand officers, job descriptions are so nuanced that you rarely get a chance to break out of your traffic beat, say, to chase down a thug.

The beauty of most trade jobs, of course, is that they rarely require a four-year degree. In fact, the best way to a blue-collar career is almost always outside the university setting through apprenticeships, on-the-job training, and certification programs. And unions, often looking to hire more workers, are frequently willing to pay for such training. In fact, the hardest thing about pursuing a trade job may be selecting the one best suited for you from the tens of thousands that exist today. Whichever job you pursue, it's likely to offer the benefits of other trade positions—steady job growth, increasing pay, union support, and sizable pensions after twenty years or more of work.

Before you saunter off to a vocational school, however, to learn the art of bricklaying, make sure you understand the pluses and minuses of blue-collar jobs. Most people who get into trade professions do so because they love the idea of working with their hands for hours on end. That can be richly rewarding at the end of the day when you walk off a job site and look back to admire the brick wall you just erected. But the labor can be arduous on many jobs, and exhaustion and injuries are simply a part of this career.

For those who do plow through, blue-collar jobs can offer high pay in outdoor environments, plus plenty of time off each year. You may not acquire the social standing of your white-collar peers, but you can certainly make as much money as they do. And when you're pulling your BMW into the driveway of your seven-hundred-thousand-dollar home at the end of the day, does the marketing executive next door really have the better job?

A house painter, working on his or her own, can make forty-five thousand dollars the first year. An auto mechanic can pull in a starting salary of more than twenty-five bucks an hour. And police officers in large cities can make seventy-five thousand after just five or six years on the force.

Apprenticeships

Apprenticeships offer probably the best method for becoming trained in a blue-collar job, not to mention the fastest track to full-time work, since companies place apprentices in jobs upon completion of the program. Each year, more than 440,000 Americans become apprentices within one of the country's thirty-seven thousand apprentice programs. The programs, operated in conjunction with unions, trade groups, government organizations, and businesses, welcome people sixteen and older interested in working in blue-collar jobs. The upshot of an apprenticeship, besides not having to pay for formal education, is that students who are enrolled in these programs (usually lasting from one to six years) get paid while they're learning, albeit at reduced rates from a full-time job. Still, it beats sitting in a classroom, shelling out thousands in tuition every semester, only to come out with knowledge of general theories but no practical experience.

Besides providing a certificate of completion in the line of work studied, many apprenticeships offer students the opportunity to obtain an associate's degree as well. If you want to become a trade employee, an apprenticeship is generally valued by employers over other forms of training, because apprenticeships tend to teach higher standards of safety than other educational methods, saving organizations money on workers' compensation claims. Graduates of these programs are also seen as more highly motivated.

POPULAR APPRENTICESHIPS AND
THEIR INCOME POTENTIAL

Job Title	Potential Hourly Wage	Why It's Popular
Electrician	$33	• Significant job growth • High demand for workers
Carpenter	$28	• Self-employment • Steady work
Plumber/pipe fitter/sprinkler fitter	$32	• One of highest-paid construction jobs • Job opportunities are excellent
Sheet metal worker	$30	• Fast job growth
Structural steel worker	$31	• Continued job growth to 2012
Elevator constructor	$36	• Consistent work schedules • Increased job growth • Largely immune to economic downturns
Roofer	$25	• Strong on-the-job training • Immense job opportunities • Largely immune to economic downturns • Self-employment
Bricklayer	$31	• Excellent job prospects • Little to no experience or training required • Self-employment
Construction laborer	$23	• Strong on-the-job training • Immense job growth
Painter	$24	• On-the-job training • Self-employment
Boilermaker	$29	• More job openings due to boomer retirement

Job Title	Potential Hourly Wage	Why It's Popular
Heating/ air-conditioning installer	$26	• Strong job growth • Consistent, year-round work
Millwright	$29	• Consistent job growth • Stronger-than-average union support
Machinist	$23	• Excellent job opportunities
Tool-and-die maker	$31	• Excellent job opportunities
Insulation worker	$26	• Excellent job opportunities

On-the-Job Training

Art Miller has held a number of trade jobs, including millwright, quarry foreman, and mechanical contractor. For none of them did he complete an apprenticeship or any formal education. "Coming out of high school, I just wanted to get away from schooling," he says. His first job as a millwright, for example, was essentially dropped in his lap when, after he left the military, a friend's father asked him about his plans for work. "I said, 'I'm not thinking that far ahead,'" Miller recalls. His friend's father suggested Miller visit the steel mill where he worked to fill out an application. Soon he was working as a millwright, making I-beams for bridges, making as much as sixty-five thousand dollars a year. Later, after transferring to another steel mill and disliking the work, Miller's boss transferred him to a quarry where he worked as a mechanical contractor, erecting conveyors and towers to move quarry materials. In that job, as in others, Miller asked questions of supervisors often, aggressively sought out new roles and responsibilities, and looked for ways to gain promotions. Those methods paid off. Currently, he's a production foreman at a quarry in Lancaster, Pennsylvania—with no college degree and no official training, other than what he received on the job. His salary is more than seventy thousand dollars a year. "For someone who goes into this work with initiative," Miller says, "they can learn entry-level jobs." Building upon those talents by observing higher-ups, asking to learn a new skill, or developing an on-the-job mentor can lead to higher pay and even management positions, like those Miller has held, both in steel mills and at quarries.

Miller was lucky in that a friend's father was connected to blue-collar work. If you have friends or family in similar positions, referrals to jobs and on-the-job training programs are still a common way to enter trade professions. "I've hired many people straight off the street, and they were able to run almost anything," says Miller. But for those who don't have connections through friends, neighbors, or relatives, taking at least one or two preliminary classes in high school or at a community college in subjects such as welding or mechanical drawing may be a wise idea. That way, you're at least familiar with some of the skills needed to work in those jobs. And it will help you build a more productive conversation with those you may meet or conduct informational interviews with people already working in that field.

In many professions, internships are available for those with little to no experience. Participating in them is a good way to start training on the job for a career in trade work, and a great way to land a permanent job with a company. For internship opportunities, contact organizations in your area. The American Federation of Labor–Congress of Industrial Organizations (AFL-CIO), www.aflcio.org, is a fine place to start—for lists of unions, job training information, and other news about working in blue-collar industries.

Associate's Degrees
and Certification Programs

These days, the nearly twelve hundred community colleges in America are quickly becoming some of the most effective training grounds for blue-collar jobs. They grant more than 490,000 associate's degrees and almost 235,000 certificates a year, many for trade professions. Obtaining a certificate or associate's degree through a community college can be an effective path to a blue-collar job. To find one in your area and take a look at its curriculum offerings, visit the Web site of the American Association of Community Colleges at www.aacc.nche.edu.

High Growth Trades

As the sample of trade jobs listed in the chart below illustrates, plenty of blue-collar jobs are projected to bring substantial growth to the job market in the next several years.

SAMPLE TRADE JOB GROWTH TO 2012

Trade Job Category	Growth Percentage	Number of New Jobs by 2012
Trucking	21	275,000
Construction	15	7.7 million
Medical manufacturing	23	68,000
Maintenance and repair	14	776,000
Transportation	13	1.3 million

Source: *Occupational Outlook Handbook*, 2004–2005

High Dollars/Low Interest

Worth mentioning here are a few jobs that offer unprecedented pay for blue-collar workers. Their only drawback: They're highly unappealing to many people. But for those who can stomach them they offer excellent pay, mostly because it's hard to recruit people to these fields of work. If you can stand it, you're likely to have plush paychecks, weeks off at a stretch, and the freedom of escaping the daily grind.

Oil Rig Worker

People who are comfortable with hunkering down many miles out in the middle of an ocean or Arctic reserve are paid handsomely for their efforts—sometimes a hundred thousand dollars a year or more. And while their jobs keep them in isolation (with only other rig workers for company), they also enjoy stretches of time off when they're back home. Interested? Check out sites such as www .oilcareer.com, www.whatoiljobs.com, or www.rigworker.com.

Hazardous Waste Remover

Job opportunities are excellent for people willing to remove asbestos, mold, nuclear materials, and lead to keep buildings safe. Turnover is rampant, due to safety concerns from workers, which means jobs are readily available. And earnings can exceed twenty-seven dollars an hour.

Crime Scene Cleaner

Yes, it's gruesome, but somebody's got to do it. Those who do either get used to the horrors of the job or leave the field in short order. No matter their duration, people who clean up crime scenes make excellent money doing so—how else would you attract workers? Yearly income can easily exceed a hundred grand. Companies like Bio-Tec Emergency Services offer information about working in this field as well as information on training and jobs; see www.usacsc.com.

Where the Blue-Collar Jobs Are

Regardless of what training path you take, finding blue-collar work can be easier in some states than others, with higher concentrations of blue-collar workers in the Southeast and Midwest. One rule to keep in mind when looking for blue-collar jobs: Everyone starts at the bottom. Particularly in unions, where hierarchy is established by years of service, you can't climb over peers and make your way up the job ladder simply by showing up and going the extra mile. Whether you slave away for sixty hours a week, giving 120 percent the whole time, or sit on your haunches refusing to lift a finger except when absolutely necessary, your union status will remain the same. Below are a smattering of general blue-collar job boards, along with specialized job sites for specific fields of work:

- ◆ Motivation Tool Chest, www.motivation-tools.com. This Web site, packed with insights and information from a former blue-collar worker, offers great information for those new to the world.
- ◆ Blue Collar And Proud Of It, www.bluecollarandproudofit .com. Want a blue-collar job? This site offers listings by specialty as well as information about apprenticeship programs.

- BlueCollarJobs.com, www.bluecollarjobs.com. This very comprehensive site allows seekers of trade work to search dozens of trade industries, post their résumés, and research various trade professions.
- EveryTruckJob.com, www.everytruckjob.com. Job opportunities are expected to be "favorable" for truck drivers in the next several years, according to the Department of Labor. And why shouldn't they be? Cabs have become plush with wood-grain interiors, spacious sleeping areas, and the latest technological advancements. It's enough to make sitting behind the wheel for hours at a stretch enjoyable. And with salaries of more than fifty grand a year, it's not a bad gig if you can get it. EveryTruckJob.com recognizes this, promoting the industry and offering job postings on its Web site.

The Big Worker in a Small Pond

For workers having a hard time making headway in the trade world through traditional routes—apprenticeships, on-the-job training, and blue-collar job boards—there is one other way that might be more effective. Working at tiny companies, mechanics' shops, and the like may offer better job options, more intricate mentoring opportunities, and the chance to do more, since smaller outfits tend to ask what staff they have to do more.

Bob Webb, a retired machinist and founder of the Web site Blue Collar World (www.motivation-tools.com/youth/blue_collar_world.html), says he job-hopped for years (a common phenomenon in some blue-collar fields), which allowed him to gain more experience faster, and boost his pay in the process, incurring a slight pay raise with each new job. At smaller shops, "they don't care about educational background," Webb insists, because they're too busy trying to produce work.

Starting trade work in this manner may mean accepting rock-bottom wages initially, but Webb says moving from job to job with regularity means steady incremental increases in pay. Averaging eighteen months at companies where he worked, Webb was often able to increase his pay by 50 percent from job to job. On occasion employers balked at his résumé, full of short-tenure jobs, but ultimately they were more concerned with the skills and experience he could bring to their workplace.

The Nontraditional Woman

For Katie Haven, working for the Alaska Marine Highway System is pretty much all or nothing. As a chief engineer for the Alaska ferries, Haven spends four weeks on the job and four weeks off. "One of the things that appealed to me was having big chunks of time off," says Haven, who's been a maritime worker for more than twenty years. "I get one day of paid vacation for every day I work. So I'm getting paid when I'm not out working." For her efforts, she makes $120,000 a year.

Haven, who is also an editor for the newsletter produced by the Women's Maritime Association, happens to have a college degree. But many women in roles similar to hers have no postsecondary education, and have landed their jobs through basic, on-the-job training or through union apprenticeships as brief as three months.

From tankers that sail worldwide to ferry systems like Haven's employer, the number of women on ships is increasing each year.

"I love the freedom," Haven says. "You're independent and not tied to anything." For those with a sense of adventure, maritime work offers travel to unusual places in different ports around the world.

Her foray into the maritime field, however, is significant for much more than adventure seeking. What was once an entirely male profession is now slowly being filled by more and more women.

That's reflective of trade work in general. Still considered non-traditional work for women (meaning less than 25 percent of those employed are female), trade professions are an extremely popular sector for many women who love working outdoors, with their hands, traveling the world, and participating in challenging physical labor.

The Modern-Day Rosie

When the working-class icon Rosie the Riveter first materialized during World War II—in songs and on posters—it seemed the time had come to welcome women into the trade professions. How quickly that idea floundered when men returned home and took back their industrial welding jobs, truck driving routes, shipyard duties, and other blue-collar work! Almost as quickly as they'd filled men's shoes, women were escorted out of the factory.

Since then, images of the dungaree-clad Rosie have continued to serve as a symbol of the working woman, but her role in the trade profession has been more or less symbolic. Still, in the past thirty years, women have slowly reclaimed their right to work in the trade jobs traditionally held by men. The numbers remain slight—only 3 percent of construction jobs go to women, for example—but they're growing. And so are the opportunities for women in the trades. In fact, some stereotypically female interests—pattern making, say—transfer well to jobs such as construction, where workers must read blueprints to complete their work. "Laying out sheet metal is very much like making a dress," says Beth Youhn, executive director of Tradeswomen, Inc., a resource and support group based in Oakland, California, for women in the trades.

For women who have no experience in trade work but are interested by the opportunities and income in the field, there are pre-apprenticeship programs designed specifically to introduce women to the world of blue-collar work. In New York, for example, NEW (Nontraditional Employment for Women) offers programs called Construction Trades Prep and Blue Collar Prep, in which women participate in hands-on work and learn about career opportunities. Still not sure blue-collar work is for you? NEW offers orientation sessions three days a week. For course offerings and additional information, visit www.new-nyc.org.

Similar organizations include:

- Wider Opportunities for Women (WOW), www .wowonline.org. WOW, a Washington, DC–based organization, is focused on creating better job opportunities for women in nontraditional jobs.
- Tradeswomen Now and Tomorrow (TNT), www .tradeswomennow.org. Launched in 1999, this group works to create more visibility for issues facing women in trade jobs, as well as recommending policies to help women seeking blue-collar jobs.
- Work4Women.org, www.work4women.org. This site focuses largely on training for nontraditional jobs,

particularly for young women and girls, with links on education, training, and interviewing for jobs.

◆ Workplace Solutions, www.workplacesolutions.org. A robust clearinghouse of news and information for women seeking jobs in nontraditional lines of work, as well as those simply wanting information about the types of jobs available to women.

If nothing else, Youhn suggests that women who may be interested in trade work start by taking carpentry, electrical, math, or other classes at their local community or junior college to get a sense of what types of skills are needed. Electricians, for instance, actually have to know algebra. So much for that ubiquitous question among high school students: "When am I ever going to use this in the real world?"

Taking classes also gives women an idea of which trade might be most interesting to them as well as which one they might be most skilled at. That's important, because unions that pay for apprenticeship programs require that entrants choose a specific line of work prior to training. At nine thousand dollars a head to train apprentices, they want to make sure they're getting a return on their investment.

Many women in trades—and men, too—pick an occupation simply because it pays more than others. A pre-apprenticeship will cover trades, their pay, and the nature of the work—all important factors to consider collectively, rather than pay alone. "People come to us and say, 'What's the trade that pays the most?'" Youhn says. "That's the wrong question, because if you're going to have to do something eight hours a day for the next thirty years, you're going to want to enjoy it. We encourage women to really do their homework."

It's also important for women to consider which trades may be more physically demanding. Even advocates for women in the trades admit there are some jobs they simply can't do. "With women, upper-body strength is sometimes an issue," Youhn says. Make sure you truly understand what's at stake in even the seemingly least laborious of jobs. Painting, for instance, usually involves much more labor than people would expect. "Women think, *I painted my bedroom. How hard can it be?*" Youhn says. "It can be hard, because you're climbing up on scaffolding with heavy buckets of paint or paint sprayers."

To boost the strength of female blue-collar workers, some training programs include weight-training and endurance-building workouts. All of this helps women gain better peace of mind as they go up against men for positions. "Twenty years ago, guys would ask me, 'Why do you want to do this?'" Youhn says, as they worked alongside her on construction sites. "Back then guys were very, very hostile, because they felt that women were taking a man's job," reducing their own work opportunities. But as more single moms enter the workplace (NEW, for example, offers help on finding child care services for working moms in the trades), men are realizing that they're going to be seeing more and more females at work sites. And their attitudes have adjusted dramatically in recent years. Says Youhn, "We have a lot more progressive guys out there these days who really appreciate what women do."

Chapter Eight

Proving Your Worth
Without a Degree

Those who don't have a college degree preceding them in their job search sometimes panic, assuming their résumé must look subpar next to their competitors'. They try to craft tricky, smoke-and-mirror responses that paint them in a better light. But often they don't need to. As the following non-college-grad demonstrates, the lack of a degree should never be a barrier to the perfect job—even if your goal is to get on national television.

Kat Carney (whom we met in chapter 1), a former health anchor for CNN, always knew the value of education. Her mother owned a bookstore. Her father was an army colonel. And the idea of Carney skipping out on college never occurred to anyone, least of all to Carney herself, who was twenty points shy of perfect on her math SAT score. She walked out of high school with a full ride to Howard University in Atlanta. Her freshman year, she plunked herself down in the middle of campus and declared herself a hotel administration major. So far, so good. Then the doubts started creeping in. "I'm not really feeling this," Carney recalls thinking about her lukewarm response to hotel administration. Pretty soon it wasn't just the major. College in general started to lose its appeal. And Carney began to realize that it never really had one in the first place. Growing up, "My dad was in the military and we were moving around a lot." As a kid, "when learning about the Leaning Tower of Pisa in school, I said, 'Oh, I've been there. I've seen the *Mona Lisa.*'" In fact Carney had seen a lot of Europe firsthand rather than through books. Doing so established a preferred way of learning for her: "I didn't understand why I would sit in school and learn when I've already been there."

In fact, Carney has always found doing, rather than studying, a much more liberating way to learn and experience life— meaning that finding a career that revolves around being free to choose where she works, how she works, and what she does on a daily basis has been crucial to her professional happiness. Those early observations would propel much of her career path later on.

Feeling stifled at Howard, Carney transferred to Georgia State her sophomore year to pursue a major that might lead her into business management within the arts. At the same time, she landed an internship at Motown Records and started taking acting classes at the city's Alliance Theater.

Combining work at Motown with school meant her days were long—from eight thirty to two thirty at Motown, followed by courses in the afternoon. "I had a lot of responsibility," Carney says. "I wasn't making coffee and faxing. I was doing promotions for a secondary market in the Southeast."

And she was loving it. But acting, promotions, and college together were too much to juggle at once. With that full of a plate, she soon realized, "something has to give." It turned

out to be college. Small acting jobs in Atlanta turned into
television commercials and eventually a move to New York,
where Carney spent six years in her midtwenties making sixty
thousand dollars a year filming commercials. A devastating ill-
ness, polycystic ovarian syndrome (PCOS), hit soon after, which
forced Carney to balloon up to 240 pounds and lose most of her
hair—and with it, her acting jobs. She spent the next few years
in Atlanta, finally hitting rock bottom in the late 1990s. Rather
than succumb, Carney changed her diet, revamped her lifestyle
(a painful road that involved baby steps to physical fitness), and
launched a Web site about the disease so other women might be
able to discuss their problems and concerns. Doing so put her
on the map as an expert. By 2001, along with her acting background, her increasingly popular Web site eventually landed her
a job interview with CNN to host the station's new health show
for a salary in the low six figures. "I was thirty-one and had
never worked in a regular job," says Carney, who remembers
being terrified of the position. "My hands were shaking the day
we went live," she says.

She has since left CNN for QVC and continues to run her
Web site, all of which places her salary well above six figures.
Carney says that by sidestepping the typical path through college and into the corporate world, she missed out on much of
the protocol young graduates learn within American business
offices.

And that might mean she's the quintessentially unprepared job
candidate—someone without a college degree who assumes her
credentials are beneath those of others. But Carney chose not
to focus on such doubts (a healthy dose of confidence helped),
instead emphasizing her strengths and experience over her lack
of a college degree.

Baby Steps

One of the things Carney does well is approach her work—and life—one small step at a time. It can be a smart way to approach the job market as well. At the height of her affliction with PCOS, Carney recalls being so depressed she spent hours on end holed up in her apartment. She did the only thing she could think of: improve through baby steps. She started with her body, figuring out how she could muster the motivation to exercise and shed the weight the disease had helped her pack on. Her first obstacle? No exercise clothes. Probably not a legitimate excuse for your average fitness trainer. Her second excuse carried more weight: "I don't like going to the gym," Carney says.

Dreading the experience, she made microscopic endeavors to better health. At first, she drove up to the gym, walked up to the gym doors, and left. The next week, she walked through the doors, then left again. "People at the front desk would say, 'Can I help you?'" Carney recalls. A week later, she mustered the energy to walk through the doors and approach a treadmill. After that, she decided to take on actual exercise in increments, such as running on the treadmill for only one minute. "That's one minute more than I did yesterday," she would tell herself.

A one-minute treadmill workout sounds ridiculous, but the point here, Carney says, was not the workout itself—it was figuring out a way to get over her inertia. "You can get to a goal if you take it at your own pace, instead of looking at a big mountain and saying, 'I don't know how to do this,'" Carney says. Allow yourself to get overwhelmed by the big-picture approach, on the other hand, and "a year later you will be right where you started from."

Start Small

For Chet Holmes, chapter 2's successful salesperson who
skipped college and made solid six-figure salaries before age
thirty, working for smaller companies was the key to not only
gaining valuable experience on a steep learning curve with
greater responsibilities in various positions, but also avoiding the issue of human resource managers asking him why he
didn't have a college degree. "IBM wouldn't hire me because I
don't have a high school diploma," he says, "let alone a college
degree. I couldn't get into more well-established companies, so I
ended up at these smaller companies."

In the end, smaller firms actually gave Holmes greater opportunity for growth and advancement. That holds true for trade work
as well. Those as yet unproven in a particular craft might find
that they get asked to take on a greater range of tasks at smaller
shops than larger companies, widening their skill sets and increasing their attractiveness and income with future employers.

Go for It

Just because you don't have a college degree doesn't mean you
should be any less assertive in the workplace. In fact, it probably means you should be *more* aggressive. That's the attitude
chapter 1's Kristin Crockett, training manager at telecom company Qwest Communications, took when launching her career.

But the most important development to Crockett, besides the
increase in responsibility, professional worth, and, of course, pay,
was that she was molding the career she wanted after discovering
her interest in HR, by strategically avoiding assignments and

positions that weren't inspiring and seeking out those that gave her roles in her career passion: corporate diversity issues.

Throughout her rise at Jones Intercable, where she eventually became the director of training and development, Crockett was certainly aware of the fact that competing job candidates often had degrees and far more formal education than she. Even though she left Jones after it was purchased by Comcast, which shut down the location, Crockett had little problem finding similar work, first at Starz Entertainment Group, the movie premium channel, and now at Qwest. But Crockett, who answered honestly when asked about her college degree ("continuing education wasn't an interest of mine, while working was"), has on occasion been apprehensive about her lack of a degree, for fear of running across an "education snob," determined to hire only college grads.

Still, the notion that some companies are unwilling to take a chance on someone without a four-year degree doesn't make sense to her, especially when most four-year degrees don't have relevance to the job a person is seeking. "I could have gotten a degree in interior design and still be where I am today," Crockett says. But for some recruiters, "If you don't have a degree, for whatever reason in their mind, you are not capable at some level." Maybe some employers would be "happy that I went to four years of college so I know how to take notes," Crockett guesses jokingly.

But her point is well taken: Plenty of firms are apprehensive about hiring applicants who don't have a college degree.

Cover the Basics

No matter what type of profession you're interested in, it's going to take a résumé, cover letter, and interviews to land the job. All of which can be daunting if you have no experience with any of them. No worries. Plenty of resources exist to help people in your very position. Read on to find out what those are and how to locate them, as well as crucial points to consider as you hunt for a job.

Writing the Résumé

If you're so new to the job search that the idea of writing a résumé leaves you cold, don't worry. There are plenty of tools to get you started. If you don't know where to start, one of the best places is online, where job boards such as Monster (www.monster.com), CareerBuilder (www.careerbuilder.com), and Yahoo! HotJobs (http://hotjobs.yahoo.com) offer plentiful tips on assembling a résumé and what to include in it. Or you can access résumé-writing Web sites such as www.10minuteresume.com, which will walk you through a step-by-step process. The service runs $59.95 for a year (let's hope your job search is shorter than that) or $9.95 per month. The site also offers a onetime free trial run to give you a sense of how its tools can help you.

Outside consultants aside, if you're game to sitting down and trying to bang out a résumé yourself, it's really not that hard. Remember to keep it clean: Bullet points have long been a résumé writer's best friend. In addition, keep narrative to a minimum, and include numbers. Numbers pop off the page amid all the words an HR professional is trying to wade through on a résumé. But more importantly, they're an effective way to demonstrate your success at previous jobs, as well as show that you're willing to stand behind your work.

Since you've skipped the college degree, you'll have to approach the educational section of your résumé in a slightly different manner than the typical applicant. That doesn't mean it's a résumé killer. In fact, for trade work, it's actually *better* to list certifications, apprenticeships, and the like. If you're entering a traditional office environment where everyone you're competing against will most likely have a college degree, set yourself apart by listing certifications, classes, or industry conferences you have attended that have given you new skills to better do the job you're applying for.

If you've been out of the workforce for a year or more, or are applying for jobs for which you have no experience, it might be smart to ditch the standard résumé with your work history listed by year, and assemble one that simply lists your abilities instead.

Let's take a look at the differences between the two styles of résumés—one set up by year, the other by abilities.

Résumé Set Up by Year

JOHN SMITH
1 Peachtree Street, Atlanta, Georgia 30303
404-123-1234 • jsmith@gmail.com

PROFESSIONAL EXPERIENCE

2003–Present   Dakati Telecom, Atlanta, GA
Southeast District Sales Manager
- Manage a staff of 30 salespeople
- Track customer service calls and compile customer satisfaction reports
- Work with marketing and sales to track customer issues
- Help create marketing materials for customer and suppliers
- Increased sales revenue by 135 percent for the past three years
- Decreased employee turnover by 25 percent

2000–2003   Dakati Telecom, Atlanta, GA
Field Sales Representative
- Promoted to sales manager
- Expanded the Southeast territory by 1,000 clients in the past three years
- Exceeded quota by 200 percent for the past three years
- Led team training seminars for new field reps
- Developed a solutions-based sales strategy to better understand client needs

1998–2000   Dakati Telecom, Atlanta, GA
Customer Service Representative
- Promoted to field sales rep
- Increased call efficiency by 20 percent with customers and suppliers
- Received outstanding customer service representative award for 2002

1997   Hilliard's Department Store
Sales Associate
- Sold merchandise in women's wear, electronics, home accessories, and jewelry departments
- Received sales associate of the month award five times
- Worked one on one with customers

EDUCATION

1998   Georgia State University, Atlanta, GA
Certificate of professional selling

2000   Dale Carnegie Sales Advantage Training
SalesForce.com CRM Fundamentals Training

Résumé Set Up by Abilities

JOHN SMITH
1 Peachtree Street, Atlanta, Georgia 30303
404-123-1234 • jsmith@gmail.com

OBJECTIVE
Sales management position allowing for executive growth, staff management, customer service, and revenue generation skills built over a seven-year career.

SKILLS SUMMARY

- CRM management
- Customer development
- Public speaking
- Revenue generation
- Compensation structures
- Budgeting
- Sales training
- Marketing
- Sales lead generation

PROFESSIONAL EXPERIENCE

Sales & Customer Service
Sales manager and business strategist with seven years of experience, doubling sales quarter to quarter. Skilled at opening new territories, overseeing customer relationship management programs, sales team performance, and turnover reduction. Experienced at building new territories and training sellers to manage new-product introductions.

Lead Generation
Proven lead generator who increased sales 135 percent with a new sales lead generation program. Directed coordination of CRM systems between marketing and customer service staffs to create a seamless customer service and sales experience.

Sales Management
Trainer of sellers with varied experience, from entry-level employees to executives. Served as mentor to underperforming staff members, and helped them turn around performance from selling 32 percent under quota to more than 55 percent above it.

EMPLOYMENT

2003–Present   Dakati Telecom, Atlanta, GA
Southeast District Sales Manager

2000–2003   Dakati Telecom, Atlanta, GA
Field Sales Representative

1998–2000   Dakati Telecom, Atlanta, GA
Customer Service Representative

1997   Hilliard's Department Store
Sales Associate

EDUCATION & TRAINING

1998   Georgia State University, Atlanta, GA
Certificate of professional selling

2000   Dale Carnegie Sales Advantage Training
SalesForce.com CRM Fundamentals Training

Crafting the Cover Letter

Just like the résumé, the cover letter should include specific information—bulleted, even—that will highlight your abilities and strengths. Include here, as you would in your résumé, actual numbers detailing accomplishments, or certifications, if applicable to the job you're applying for.

Yes, the letter is an opportunity to tout your talent and experience, but it's also an opportunity to let the company know you understand its business, are well versed on its industry, and have the specific skills needed for the job. Make sure you include the abilities you have that match specific needs mentioned in the job description. An effective cover letter might read something like this:

Mr. David Jones
Boyden Pharmaceuticals
123 Medical Way
Washington, DC 20001

Dear Mr. Jones:

With the rapid pace of health care innovations today, it's crucial that your company have competent sellers introducing your products to the market, but who can understand and explain in great detail how those products can help physicians better diagnose and treat their patients.

My 12-year history in the medical sales market has prepared me for a position with your company as Northwest regional manager. My experience includes:

- Increasing sales by 135 percent for the last three quarters at my last company.
- Closing the first 7-figure piece of business in the company's history.
- Training sellers to introduce new products to expanding territories.

In addition, I'm accomplished at coordinating marketing and CRM projects. I am looking for a position that would help me build upon these accomplishments in a challenging environment.

I have enclosed my résumé for your review. I look forward to an opportunity to speak to you about positions available at Boyden Pharmaceuticals. I will follow up with you in a week to determine if we might set up a meeting at your convenience.

Thank you for your consideration.

Sincerely,

Tom Patterson

Nailing the Interview

Now that you've written an impressive cover letter, detailed your credentials on your résumé, and managed to get on an employer's calendar for an interview, there are a few final preparations to make before the meeting, as well as some things to keep in mind during the interview.

Before the Fact

First of all, do your research. Too many people look at a job posting, create responses to match the described responsibilities, and never conduct due diligence on the company itself or its larger role in the industry in which it operates. Blue-collar workers can likely get away without this, since employers are more concerned with their practical skills than their understanding of the company's business strategy. But even trade workers are better served by conducting research, which can give them insight into current and future job opportunities based upon the company's performance within its industry and the projected growth and emerging career opportunities of an industry as a whole.

Another key is to write down your professional strengths and examples of work experiences that illustrate those strengths. Writing it down, rather than running over these in your head, is key: Most of us are more likely to remember something we've written.

Next, do some role-playing. Ask a friend, family member, or any one else who might be available to run through a practice interview. Many people sit alone in their homes practicing answers out loud to themselves. That's a start, but until you're sitting face-to-face with another individual, you can't really get a sense of the stress of an interview. Even though the interviewer may be your boyfriend during practice, having another person there to actually run you through the paces is far more realistic and helpful than memorizing answers on your own.

And of course, be presentable. Even entry-level positions in the most casual settings require proper attire. We'd all like to think we're being judged solely on our professional merits, but the reality is that first impressions speak volumes. When an editor at a trade publishing company interviewed candidates a few years ago, one candidate practiced such poor hygiene, and left such a foul odor in the room, that the editor decided to cut the interview short—spending half as much time with the offensively presented applicant. Needless to say, he didn't get the job.

In the Hot Seat

Nervous about your interview? Welcome to the club. Even the most seasoned job hunters can experience a racing heart and sweaty palms when meeting with company recruiters and interviewers. But there are plenty of ways to help limit any anxiety that might creep up during the interview.

Remember, an interview is really just a conversation in which an applicant and an employer learn more about each other to determine if they're a fit. Try to think of the experience as a professional conversation rather than a grilling in the hot seat. Of course, depending on the job and the interviewer's style, this approach will be easier to apply in some places than others.

Furthermore, like all conversations, this one is a two-way street. Yes, this is a chance for you to impress potential employers. But it's also their chance to do the same. Remember, they *want* people like you who have the knowledge and talent to make their business better. They need you as much as you need them. And leveling the interviewing playing field is crucial to lessening interview anxiety.

Many career experts advise trying to make a personal connection with the HR professional sitting across from you. That's not a bad idea, but don't connect for connection's sake. Try to pick up on something that you would genuinely be interested in discussing. If you're a Pittsburgh native, commenting on the Steelers hat on your interviewer's desk is fine. If they've just won the Super Bowl but you don't know the difference between a touchdown and a field goal, your lack of NFL knowledge could not only make the interviewer question your knowledge in general, but make you seem disingenuous in the process. The best thing to do? Just try to be as informal as possible while still remaining professional.

Finally, here's a trick familiar among public speakers: Forcibly slowing down your voice will cause your body to do the same. If you hear yourself racing to get through an answer, pause, then continue at a much slower rate. That also gives you time to think more clearly and carefully about your answer and the information you want to deliver to the person you're meeting with.

Thrown for a Loop

Interviewing styles vary widely and, because they're often a result of an individual's personality, are highly unpredictable. Unless you have the opportunity to chat by phone with the actual person you'll be meeting with during the interview, you won't know how his or her style of interaction and engagement might affect the interviewing process. And for those who don't have a college degree, especially when competing with those who do, you may be called upon to prove your talent and ability, despite your lack of education. With that in mind, consider the following possible questions below as well as some sample answers to keep HR personnel interested.

Question: I noticed you don't have a college degree. Why not?
Possible Response: Well, I considered going to college, but I've always felt that gaining real world experience is an equally effective educational tool. In fact, after high school, I was interested in becoming a chef, so I interned at three restaurants in my city. I wanted to make sure I got a true sense of what it's like to work in that industry. For one restaurant, I got up at 4 AM and arrived at work by 5 AM, to help make the day's bread. Being extremely thorough in my job is very important to me.
Why It Works: It not only answers the interviewer's question, but takes the interview one step further by showcasing an example of your initiative.

Question: You don't have quite as much experience as we're looking for. Why should we hire you?
Possible Response: That is true, but I do have experience adapting quickly to new work environments and management styles. At my last job, I worked under three different managers, all of whom felt comfortable giving me more responsibility than my job entailed, because they trusted that I could pick up the skills for the task quickly. In addition, I'm currently enrolled in a certificate program that specifically addresses the skills needed for this job that were mentioned in your job listing. [Only say this, of course, if it's in fact the case.]
Why It Works: Poor employee retention costs US businesses millions of dollars a year. The last thing companies want is to hire someone who decides to quit three months later after

realizing the job isn't suitable. Proving your adaptability can put some of those corporate fears to rest.

Question: You seem to have some major gaps in your work experience. Why is that?

Possible Response: I reached a crossroads in my previous job, where I wasn't sure if I wanted to continue in that industry or not. Rather than jump randomly into a new position that I wasn't sure about pursuing, I decided I needed to take some time off and carefully consider my career options—including the alternative professions that might interest me most. But I wasn't sitting home thinking about that in front of the TV. I decided it would be better to volunteer at several organizations as well as take a couple of classes to get a better sense of several fields. At the same time, I received an amazing offer to spend nine months with a friend and her family in Spain. I decided to accept their offer, because I feel that exposing yourself to new cultures and places makes you a more well-rounded individual, particularly if you can learn a second language. I really think these kinds of experiences give you added perspective that can be applied to all aspects of your life, including your profession. Plus, I have to be honest, I studied Spanish for two years in high school and I've always wanted to immerse myself in the culture and better learn the language. It allowed me to improve my Spanish so much that I was nearly fluent by the time I left.

Why It Works: You've given concrete, responsible answers about why you have a gap in your work history—very few employers would question someone's thoughtfulness about their career choices. By talking about classes and volunteering experiences, you've shown that you have initiative.

Many companies put a premium on a second language these days, as well as any additional insight into other cultures. Finally, saying straight out that you simply wanted to indulge a personal desire shows your honesty—a trait every employer values.

Whatever responses you end up using to tough questions, make sure your answer is earnest, and what you genuinely feel and believe, not what you think the person on the other side of the table wants to hear. Never lie about—or even fudge—your credentials or background. Besides being unethical and general poor practice, it's likely to get you tripped up if you forget what you've already told the interviewer (nerves can quickly cloud memories) and make your story seem spotty.

One thought to keep in mind: Canned answers sound robotic or prepared—and they're easy to pick up on. Employers want people who can think on the spot, no matter the position. Don't go into interviews with memorized answers to these or other questions. Practicing such responses is simply a way to help grow comfortable with the interviewing process and become aware of the types of issues that might surface during your interview. That said, one tactic experts who are interviewed on TV use is to start thinking of their answer before the question is finished. Once you get an idea of what the question is, you can start formulating your response, so your answer seems quick and assured when you deliver it.

Following Up

Make sure to send a note—either via e-mail or, preferably, handwritten—following the interview to thank the person for speaking with you. You'd be surprised how many people don't. Doing so can certainly help you stand out. Plus, thank-you notes offer one more opportunity to remind employers of the skills and experience that make you an ideal candidate for the job. That doesn't mean you have to take it as far as Dana Korey did. She once tried to gain attention before an MTV interview by sending homing pigeons in a Victorian bird cage to the company's Chicago headquarters with the message, "Look forward to meeting at three; confirm by setting this messenger free." She got the meeting, but not the job.

Hopefully, the message is clear by now: A college degree is certainly not the only path to wealth. In fact, it's potentially the path to aimlessness. Whatever course you take in finding the best job for you, make sure you look at the big picture (*Will this job be compelling and offer growth over the long haul?*) as well as the daily details (*Will I be generally turned on by the tasks required to do this job day in and day out?*). Pay for any position will generally keep rising if you're a hard worker and top performer, which often results from enjoying what you do.

Appendix A

Helpful Career Sites

www.careerbuilder.com. One of the Web's largest online job boards, CareerBuilder is an all-purpose job search site where job seekers can look for virtually any type of position by industry or company. The site also offers career fairs at various sites around the country.

www.monster.com. Like CareerBuilder, Monster is a behemoth job board offering listings for thousands of jobs nationwide. It features loads of advice to job seekers of all ages, in various fields of interest. Monster offers specific help while hunting for your job, such as résumé-writing services, and also offers a networking search tool: Enter your location and field of interest and find other people within your area in similar lines of work.

www.zoomjobs.com. Besides general job listings, this savvy Web site offers unusually strategic job hunting advice, such as how to land interviews through direct mail. The site also serves as a vast resource of other job sites and publications, listing positions from hundreds of newspapers, trade magazines, and job banks.

www.craigslist.org. Looking for any job in any city? Check out craigslist. It's a hodgepodge of classified advertising, and, because of its offbeat listings, it offers amazing career opportunities in nearly every field imaginable.

www.quintcareers.com. A ten-year-old Web site that offers "2,500 pages" of career advice and tips, including a series of articles with detailed tips regarding job hunting.

www.vault.com. Want to find out about an industry? This is a great place to start. Vault.com offers synopsis of industries, trends, job offerings, and even entrepreneurship.

www.hcdonline.com. Want to read the latest Hollywood script—and get paid for it? That's the kind of job available at the Hollywood Creative Directory. The Web site also provides insight about the entertainment industry and how to land jobs within it.

www.6figurejobs.com. You might think that jobs that qualify for listing on this Web site would definitely require a college degree. What they really require, however, is experience. And not all positions are that high up the corporate ladder, which means recruiters on this site are looking for ability, not diplomas, while offering lucrative incomes.

www.thingamajob.com. This national staffing Web site sponsored by Allegis Group lists jobs by category and state. It's very easy to navigate.

www.tribe.net lists a random smattering of jobs (almost like a craigslist job board) for positions in your city—from nutritionist to carpenter.

www.jobwarehouse.com. Besides access to more than sixteen thousand jobs and twenty-four hundred hiring managers, JobWarehouse.com also offers general employment news as well as news about developments within specific companies.

www.careermag.com. A great site for those who are conducting general job searches. It lists thousands of jobs searchable by industry, as well as reports on the health of those industries. In addition, it also offers visitors a career resource link with information on everything from student loan consolidation to continuing education.

www.careerlab.com. No specific job postings here. Instead, this site offers every resource on career development a job seeker may need, including a cover letter library with dozens of samples.

www.thehighschoolgraduate.com. If you're approaching high school graduation and you still have no idea what to do with your career, you're not alone. Luckily, this Web site will help you sort through the options with information on career training programs, the military, and more. In addition, the site lists reference articles on dozens of topics.

Finally, for a helpful salary calculator, visit www.homefair.com/homefair/calc/salcalc.html?NETSCAPE_LIVEWIRE.src=Espan.

Appendix B

Additional Reading

Success Without College. Linda Lee. Doubleday, 2000.

Unfocused Kids: Helping Students to Focus on Their Education and Career Plans. Suzy Mygatt Wakefield, Howard Sage, Doris Rhea Coy, and Tami Palmer. CAPS Press, 2004.

Secrets of the Young and Successful: How to Get Everything You Want Without Waiting a Lifetime. Jennifer Kushell with Scott M. Kaufman. Fireside, 2003.

The Uncollege Alternative: Your Guide to Incredible Careers and Amazing Adventures Outside College. Danielle Wood. ReganBooks, 2000.

America's Top 100 Jobs for People Without a Four-Year Degree. Ron and Caryl Krannich. Impact Publications, 2005.

Success Without a College Degree: Dissolving the Roadblocks Between You and Success. John T. Murphy. Achievement Dynamics, 2001.

The Blue Collar Resume and Job Hunting Guide: Secrets to Getting the Job You Really Want. Ron Krannich. Impact Publications, 2006.

Hard-Hatted Women: Life on the Job. Molly Martin and Sandy Thacker. Avalon Publishing Group, 1997.

Cool Careers for Dummies, 2nd edition. Marty Nemko and Paul and Sarah Edwards. Wiley Publishing Inc., 2001.

The Gap Year Advantage: Helping Your Child Benefit from Time Off Before or During College. Karl Haigler and Rae Nelson. St. Martin's Press, 2005.

Gap Years for Grown Ups. Susan Griffith. Vacation Work Publications (UK), 2004.

202 High Paying Jobs You Can Land Without a College Degree. Jason R. Rich. Entrepreneur Press, 2006.

Sales Careers: The Ultimate Guide to Getting a High-Paying Sales Job. Edward R. Newill and Louise M. Kursmark. JIST Works Inc., 2003.

Index

WOW (Wider Opportunities for
    Women), 159

Y
Yahoo! Hot Jobs, 168
Youhn, Beth, 159, 160, 161

Z
Zimmerman, Bernie, 33
Zoomjobs.com, 181
Zuberbuhler, Jim, xviii, 7, 60, 61
Zweben, Stuart, 108